Grant Thornton

SMART TAX TIPS

Winning Strategies to Reduce Your 1998 Taxes

turnerbooks.

Toronto

Canadian Cataloguing in Publication Data

Grant Thornton
    Smart tax tips ... winning strategies to reduce your 1998 taxes

Annual.
1999–
ISSN 1481-111
ISBN 1-55228-024-1 (1999 issue)

1. Income tax—Law and legislation—Canada.
I. Grant Thornton (Firm)

HJ4661.G77   343.7105'2'05   C98-900795-2

We acknowledge the financial support of the Government of Canada through the Book Publishing Industry Development Program for our publishing activities.

turnerbooks.
1670 Bayview Avenue, Suite 310
Toronto, Ontario
M4G 3C2
(416) 489-2188

We've made every effort to ensure the information included in this text is accurate, but no publication should be used as a substitute for competent professional advice in implementing tax-planning decisions. We invite our readers to contact any of our Grant Thornton offices across Canada to meet with one of our tax advisers to discuss your specific tax situation.

Readers should be aware that the commentary in this book is based on the Income Tax Act and all pending draft legislation and regulations issued by the Department of Finance as of June 30, 1998. Post-publication changes may have a material effect on the recommendations in this book. Please consult with your tax adviser to learn of relevant changes to the legislation.

ACKNOWLEDGEMENTS

Smart Tax Tips - Winning Strategies to Reduce Your 1998 Taxes has been compiled and written by tax advisers and other professionals from Grant Thornton.

Key contributions have been made by:
  Steve Roth - National Service Line Leader, Tax
  Cathy Stam, Senior Manager, National Tax
  David Blom, Dartmouth
  Chris Britton, Dartmouth
  Don Carroll, New Westminister
  Patrick Cunningham, Fredericton
  Gary Dent, Toronto
  John Granelli, Winnipeg
  Nora Gubins, National
  Cathy Kuhrt, Toronto
  Patricia Macdonald, National
  Keith MacIntyre, Dartmouth
  Sean Tait, Toronto
  Don Wolsey, Halifax
  Karen Yull, Hamilton
  Lucie Laliberté, Montreal, Raymond Chabot Grant Thornton
  William Zink, Chicago, Grant Thornton LLP

You may contact any of the contributors listed above through our Website at www.GrantThornton.ca

INTRODUCTION

In Canada, there are two things we always seem to constantly debate — the weather and taxes. There may not be anything we can do about the weather, but there is a lot that can be done about your taxes.

That's why Grant Thornton, one of Canada's leading firms of chartered accountants and business advisers, developed *Smart Tax Tips*. This insightful, easy-to-understand book cuts through the clutter and confusion to provide the strength of advice on taxes and Canada's tax rules. This book presents the information you need for your personal or business tax strategies in a quick and easy-to-find manner. Our smart tips will save you time, money and worry — at tax time and throughout the entire year.

Smart Tax Tips is a product of the wisdom and experience of the tax experts at Grant Thornton. With 45 offices serving communities across Canada, our firm has been helping owner-managed businesses, public sector managers and not-for-profit organizations achieve their goals for more than 50 years.

If you are a business owner, corporate manager, employee, budding entrepreneur, home-based business owner, a stay-at-home parent without income, a retiree on a fixed income, or one of the number of Canadians who needs tax help, then *Smart Tax Tips* is for you.

Whatever your situation, whatever questions you might have about eligible deductions, taxes on investments, tax credits and much more, *Smart Tax Tips* will guide you through. *Smart Tax Tips* has more than 100 practical tips to assist you with your tax-planning strategies and to help you legally minimize the amount of tax you pay.

Smart Tax Tips will help you understand the tax environment in Canada, and instil the confidence you need to effectively and intelligently discuss the "how and why" of your tax situation when working with your tax adviser.

READER'S GUIDE

Most Canadians have come to recognize that the government often likes to do things in a big way, and the Income Tax Act is no exception. A volume of more than 2,000 pages, it presents a daunting challenge to even those familiar with Canada's tax system.

To help you avoid spending hours — maybe even days — poring over the contents of the Act in search of information pertinent to your circumstances, *Smart Tax Tips* has been designed to help you get to the heart of the matter and provide you with sound, useful information. Here's how to get the best out of this publication.

This book has been formatted so that whatever your situation might be, whatever questions you might have, you can retrieve an answer and appropriate guidance. It is not primarily intended as a beginning-to-end read.

First, there is a comprehensive index that allows you to quickly find the items relevant to your search. More than 135 topics are covered, and the index will point you to the one, two, three or more articles that relate to your interest. An important note to remember while reading the articles is that any discussion regarding the Goods and Services Tax (GST) also includes the Harmonized Sales Tax (HST) that is in place in Nova Scotia, New Brunswick, Newfoundland and Labrador.

Second, many of the articles include examples — a sample calculation or perhaps a typical scenario — to help you better understand the way certain rules work.

Third, we feature a **Top Ten Tax Tip List** that highlights some of more important aspects of strategic tax planning — each one referenced to its appropriate article.

And last, but in no way least, is this book's reason for being — the Tax Tips themselves. Throughout the book there are more than 100 tips. They can help you reduce your taxes in most cases and also avoid costly tax pitfalls that can arise at times through inadequate tax planning.

We have also included a glossary to help clarify various terms, relevant tax tables plus a tax calendar to help you plan your 1998 tax return. You will also find a list of Grant Thorton offices throughout Canada, and a form to request up-to-date tax and business advisory information from Grant Thornton via our newsletter, *Catalyst*.

Of course, with a publication this size, it is virtually impossible to include every tax rule on the books in Canada. What we have attempted to do, though, is cover the rules that most commonly arise — rules that have implications for most people in everyday business and/or their personal financial situations.

However, *Smart Tax Tips* should not be seen as a substitute for competent professional tax advice. Tax planning is a complex process that must be related to your individual circumstances.

What this book can do is give you the familiarity with the tax landscape in Canada to furnish you with an important resource — the knowledge to confidently discuss your tax status with your professional tax adviser.

There is no need to be intimidated when it comes to tax rules. Understanding them is the first step. To that end, we trust that you will find this book exceedingly beneficial.

TOP TEN TAX TIPS

1. **Maximize your RRSP contributions.** Amounts contributed to your RRSP are deductible from income. As well, tax is deferred on all amounts earned inside your RRSP until you begin receiving an RRSP retirement income **(see article 41)**.

2. **Make your interest expense tax-deductible.** If you must borrow, try to borrow for investment or business purposes before you borrow for personal reasons. The interest paid on these loans is fully deductible, while interest on personal borrowing is not **(see article 104)**.

3. **Split income with your spouse and children.** Most couples will pay less tax overall if each partner earns some of the family's investment income, rather than one partner earning it all **(see article 77)**. You can also split income with your children by acquiring capital property with a low yield but high capital gains potential in the names of your children **(see article 74)**.

4. **Ensure computer systems are Year 2000 Compliant.** Review your computer systems now to ensure that they are Year 2000 compliant. Enhanced tax deductions may be available to small- and medium-sized businesses that incur computer-related expenses **(see article 11)**.

5. **Crystallize the $500,000 capital gains deduction.** If you own and operate a business that has increased in value, plan on claiming this deduction as soon as possible. You don't have to sell your business to make a claim **(see article 92)**.

6. **Claim reserves on sales of capital assets.** If you sell capital assets but the full proceeds of sale are not receivable by year-end, you can bring the taxable portion of the capital gain into income over a five-year period (10 years for small businesses or farm property) **(see article 95)**.

7. **Realize losses to offset gains.** If you have realized capital gains in the year and have accrued losses on other investments, consider selling your losers before year-end **(see article 96)**.

8. **Reduce net income to avoid OAS clawback.** Defer income to a future year or maximize your deductions this year, so that your net income is reduced and the Old Age Security clawback is minimized **(see article 54)**.

9. **Defer tax with the RRIF minimum income option.** Registered retirement income funds (RRIFs) are the most flexible RRSP retirement income option and, if used wisely, can reduce your tax bill **(see article 53)**.

10. **Transfer gains to next generation with an estate freeze.** Whether you own a business or substantial investment assets, an estate freeze can minimize your future tax liability **(see article 87)**.

Contents

In This Section

Business

Whether you are a sole proprietor or an owner of a multimillion-dollar business, no one has to tell you that sound tax planning is a vital component to a healthy bottom line. And, as a successful business owner, you also recognize how essential it is to use expert professional tax advice to ensure your tax strategies are right on the money.

Understanding how Revenue Canada's tax rules work and how they might apply to your particular business circumstance will go a long way to helping you work more effectively with your tax adviser to develop both short- and long-term approaches that are beneficial to your company.

In this section, not only will you discover a number of tax tips you can apply to improve your tax profile, but you will also find 37 pertinent items that address the most common tax situations likely to affect the operation of your business.

This section includes information about the various deductions allowed, as well as what you need to know about the Goods and Services Tax. Also outlined are the measures recently introduced by the Department of Finance to alleviate some of the expenses expected to arise as businesses strive to ensure their computer systems are Year 2000 compliant.

As well, this section covers the rules involved with eligible expenses — what you can deduct and what you cannot, whether it's the cost of business entertainment or operating a vehicle. Other featured areas include depreciation, deferrals, business investment tax credits, inventory issues, business losses, running a home office, and much more.

1. ARE YOU SELF-EMPLOYED?

As a self-employed individual, you have many more options for tax planning than if you are an employee. So it makes a lot of economic sense to clearly establish that status. Determining whether you are self-employed or employed is not always cut and dried, though. It all depends on your particular circumstances, and often comes down to how much control the person paying for your services exercises over your work.

For example, if a person (or company) controls your work hours, where you perform the work, and provides all the equipment, supplies and office help that you need, you are likely the employee element in an employer-employee equation. On the other hand, if you provide services to a number of different parties and are in a position to prioritize their demands, you will likely be considered self-employed.

Real estate agents

One area in which Revenue Canada appears to have a clear administrative policy on self-employment is if you are a real estate agent. It considers you self-employed if you are entitled to the full amount of gross commissions, and you either pay:

a. a realistic fixed amount to your broker for administrative and operating costs on a monthly, annual or other basis; or

b. a percentage of your gross commissions to your broker to realistically cover such costs, and you set your own commission rate for sales on your listings.

2. YOUR YEAR-END

Not long ago, if you were carrying on a business as a proprietor or as a member of a partnership, you (or the partnership) were allowed to establish any fiscal year-end for the business. That meant you were not required to select the December 31 calendar year-end, as all individual employed taxpayers must do.

Business income reported for a particular calendar year was income (or your share of the partnership income) earned up to your fiscal year-end during that specific calendar year. For example, many self-employed taxpayers chose a January 31 year-end. Business income earned from February 1, 1994, to January 31, 1995, did not have to be reported until you filed your 1995 return in 1996. That way, you could defer almost one year's income. That was until 1995 and that year's federal budget.

New rules

Since then, all sole proprietors, certain partnerships, and professional corporations that are members of affected partnerships are now required to have a December 31 year-end. If your fiscal year began any time during 1995, it would have to close on December 31, 1995. After that, of course, your fiscal year began on New Year's Day and ended the following December 31.

Partnerships affected by this include those in which at least one member is an individual, a professional corporation, or another partnership subject to this rule. (A professional corporation is any corporation that carries on the professional practice of a tax professional, dentist, lawyer, medical doctor, veterinarian or chiropractor.)

You may be able to opt out

Some taxpayers who want to have an off-calendar year-end may be eligible to use an "alternative method" of calculating income for tax purposes, whereby income is determined using a pro rata formula that adjusts income earned during the fiscal period to a calendar-year basis.

Eligible taxpayers include individuals and partnerships in which all members are individuals. This election is not available to a partnership that is a member of another partnership. If the business is carried on by a partnership, the partnership must make this election with Revenue Canada.

If you were carrying on business in 1995, this election had to be made when you filed your 1995 tax return. Otherwise, a December 31 fiscal year-end was required. And, once a December 31 fiscal year-end has been adopted, you cannot revert to the alternative method.

Those of you starting a new business, and who would like to employ a non-December 31 year-end, are strongly urged to contact your tax adviser to determine your eligibility and whether this strategy is of any advantage to you.

Something in reserve

If you had to switch to a December 31 year-end, or make adjustments to your non-calendar year income as though you had a calendar year-end, you may have had to report business income from at least two fiscal periods in your 1995 income tax return.

If this was the case, there is some relief. You were entitled to defer the excess income resulting from the change (i.e., the income from your fiscal period commencing in 1995 to December 31, 1995, or estimate thereof) over a 10-year period by claiming a reserve.

Claiming the maximum reserve each year means 5% of this excess income would have been included in income in 1995. After that, 10% of that excess would be included in each of the next eight years (1996 – 2003), and the remaining 15% would be included in income for the year 2004.

EXAMPLE

Reporting a reserve

Your unincorporated business had a January 31 year-end and earned $120,000 in the period ended January 31, 1995. Then, from February 1, 1995, to the period ended December 31, 1995, your business earned $100,000.

Assuming you did not elect to retain the January year-end (the "alternative method"), you would have to report income of $125,000 for 1995, which is $120,000 for the period ended January 31, 1995, and 5% of the $100,000 earned in the period ended December 31, 1995. In each year from 1996 to 2003, income of $10,000 will have to be included. And finally in 2004, you have to include income of $15,000. The deferral ceases to be available if you do not carry on business at the beginning of the year.

▶ *TAX TIP*
The amount of reserve claimed each year is optional – provided you include the minimum amount required in income. There may be reasons for including more income in a particular year than the minimum amount required.

▶ *TAX TIP*
Contemplating a transaction that may affect your status, such as incorporating your sole proprietorship, forming a partnership, leaving one partnership to join another, or retiring? Look before you leap and talk with your tax adviser to review the potential impact your move might have on the deferral.

If you elected to retain your non-December 31 year-end under the "alternative method" for income tax purposes, and were also using that period for individual goods and services tax (GST) reporting, you will not have to change your GST reporting. However, you have to inform Revenue Canada of this decision. If you moved to a December 31 year-end for income tax purposes, you will automatically have the same period for GST purposes.

3. TAXING PARTNERSHIP INCOME

As a member of a partnership, you must report your share of the partnership's profit or loss for the fiscal period ended in 1998. Your 1998 tax return may also have to include income as a result of claiming a transitional reserve in 1995 **(see article 2)**. While you can normally claim your share of partnership losses against your other sources of income, this may not always be the case if you are a member of a limited partnership **(see article 106)**.

Allocation of partnership income or losses is normally left up to the partners to resolve. But, if Revenue Canada determines that allocation is unreasonable, it may disallow your allocation and substitute what it considers to be a more reasonable one. For example, if you provide the capital and do most of the work in your business while your spouse contributes significantly less, you can expect Revenue Canada to disallow a 50:50 allocation of the business's income between the two of you.

Expenses that are deductible
Expenses incurred outside the partnership may be deductible. If you borrowed money to invest in the partnership, the interest on that loan is generally deductible. Any expenses that you personally incur in the course of carrying on the partnership business (e.g., promotional and automobile expenses) are also deductible. However, meal and enter-

tainment expenses are only partly deductible **(see article 14)**, and some automobile expenses may also be limited **(see article 16)**.

A partnership with more than five partners at any time during its fiscal period is required to file information returns with Revenue Canada. By the same token, a partnership with fewer than six partners must also file an information return if one of the partners is in another partnership. Each partner must receive an information slip from the partnership, outlining his or her share of partnership income and other items allocated from the partnership.

4. TO INCORPORATE OR NOT

Should you consider the possibility of transferring your business to a corporation? Well, it depends on your circumstances and the amount of income you earn. If you are currently carrying on a business as a proprietor or in a partnership, it's worth taking a look at. And the first step should be talking it over with your tax adviser, crunching the numbers and examining the viability and advantages of being incorporated.

Business income earned as a proprietor or partner is subject to income tax at your personal marginal rates. In successful years, you must pay proportionately more income tax, as the extra income places you in a higher tax bracket. However, if you can conduct your business within a corporation, up to $200,000 of taxable income per year may be taxed at a relatively low rate **(see article 5)**.

Incorporate tax-free

Your business can be transferred to a corporation without incurring income taxes on the transfer. But there are some rules that apply, which means you must follow definite procedures and meet specific criteria. Your tax adviser can advise you on the merits of incorporation, and how it might be accomplished on a tax-deferred basis.

Also, you must remember to consider the impact of incorporation on the deferral claimed for 1995 business income **(see article 2)**. At the same time, you will have to address GST considerations, although as a general rule, most sales of businesses are now not subject to GST **(see article 36)**. In conjunction, property transfer tax, retail sales tax and other non-tax issues must also examined.

Remuneration

Now that you are incorporated be aware that the corporation's profits are not yours to take. The corporation is a separate legal entity. To extract funds, you must either receive a dividend from the corporation or have it pay you a salary. In addition, if you have loaned money to your company, you can arrange to receive interest on your loan. Careful analysis is needed to calculate the best mix of salary, interest and/or dividends for your specific circumstances.

EXAMPLE

Pay less tax

Using 1998 tax rates, if as a sole proprietor you earn business income that is taxed at the top marginal rate in Ontario, you will pay approximately 50% tax. However, the same income earned by your corporation, taxed at the small business rate and distributed to you in the form of a dividend, will be subject to a combined tax of approximately 47%. This rate will vary depending on the province in which you reside and conduct business.

5. THE SMALL BUSINESS DEDUCTION

Canadian-controlled private corporations (CCPCs) are entitled to claim a small business deduction on active business income earned in Canada. The definition of "active income" is generally intended to exclude corporations created to earn what would otherwise be considered investment or employment income of the individual shareholder. Rates vary from province to province but this deduction produces a rate of tax that is from 22% to 27% lower than the general rate. The lower rate applies to annual income up to $200,000.

EXAMPLE

Lower tax rate

Suppose a CCPC, earning income from an active business carried on in Canada, has taxable income of $300,000 for its 1998 taxation year. The income eligible for the small business deduction (i.e., up to $200,000) will be taxed at the lower rate of tax and the remaining $100,000 will be taxed at the general corporate tax rate. Using federal tax rates only, income eligible for the small business deduction will be taxed at a rate of 13.12% whereas income taxed at the general corporate rate will be taxed at a rate of 29.12%.

Restrictions do apply

For any tax year ending after June 30, 1994, larger corporations will find access to this rate restricted. The restriction applies to CCPCs whose taxable capital — generally equal to a company's retained earnings, share capital and long-term debt — exceeds $10 million for the preceding year. If the taxable capital is between $10 million and $15 million, the amount eligible for the low rate is reduced from the maximum of $200,000. Any eligibility ceases if taxable capital surpasses $15 million.

Special rules apply to corporations that are associated for income tax purposes with other corporations (**see article 22**).

6. DEFERRED SALARIES

Rules relating to unpaid salaries have become quite complex, and for the most part, the rules are intended to match the timing of the employer's deduction for paying the salary with the employee's reporting of income. For example, if at the end of 1998 an employee is entitled to receive an amount in 1999 or later, and one of the main purposes for this arrangement is to defer or postpone taxation, the amount will be taxed as a benefit to the employee in 1998. This is referred to as a "salary deferral arrangement."

Exclusions

Some plans are excluded from this classification — arrangements to fund certain employee leaves of absence, for example. The rules also do not apply to bonuses paid within three years following the end of the year in which the amount became payable. But be aware, if the bonus is not paid within 179 days from the end of the employer's taxation year, the employer will not be able to deduct the amount until the year it is paid.

▶ *TAX TIP*

If a corporation's year-end comes after July 6, the company can deduct the bonus in the current year and the employee gets a tax deferral to the next year. However, the corporation must declare the bonus as of its year-end, and not pay it out until after December 31. Again, the bonus must be paid within 179 days of the year-end to be deductible.

7. LOANS FROM YOUR CORPORATION

As mentioned in article 4, you can withdraw funds from your company by paying yourself either a salary or a dividend. As well, you can access funds via a loan. The rules are quite complex and before you undertake any such measure be sure to thoroughly go over this remuneration strategy with your tax adviser to ensure that the tax avoidance rules in this area will not be violated.

Repayment timing critical

Loans that are not repaid within one year from the end of the year in which they were made will have to be reported as income for the year the loan was made. For example, you borrow $10,000 from your company on June 1, 1998. If your company has a September 30 year-end and the loan remains unpaid on September 30, 1999, you must report the $10,000 as income for the 1998 taxation year.

Some exceptions apply

Shareholders who are also employees can be excepted from the above rules. Only some types of loans are acceptable, such as a loan that enables you or your spouse to purchase a home. Other types of loans available to you include those that allow you to acquire treasury stock in your company (or a related company), or finance an automobile to be used in performing your employment duties. To qualify for one of these exceptions, bona fide arrangements must be made, at the time the loan is taken out, to repay it within a reasonable period of time. Also, to qualify for the exception from the general rule, loans made after April 26, 1995, must be attributable to your position as an employee and not because of your shareholder status.

Another exception is if lending money is part of your company's ordinary business. This being the case, the loan will be excepted from the general rule, again provided you make bona fide arrangements to repay the loan at the time the money is borrowed.

One more exception

As a relieving provision, an exception to the general rule covers loans made to an employee who is not a "specified employee," provided bona fide arrangements are made when the funds are borrowed to repay the debt within a reasonable time period. A specified employee is generally a shareholder who owns 10% or more of the shares of the employer corporation or who does not deal at arm's length with the employer corporation. But be forewarned, if anyone related to you holds shares in the company, Revenue Canada will deem you to be the owner of these shares for purposes of assessing the 10% rule.

"Excepted" loans do not have to be included in your income, but you may have to report a taxable interest benefit for the entire period that the loan is outstanding **(see article 113).**

▶ *TAX TIP*

The exception for non-specified employees applies retroactively to loans made during or after the 1990 taxation year. If you received a shareholder loan during that time and it was included in your income and you were not considered a specified employee, talk to your tax adviser – you may be eligible for a tax reduction.

8. PAYING YOUR SPOUSE AND/OR CHILDREN

Salaries paid to your spouse and/or children are tax deductible to your business as long as their services are actually performed and the wages are reasonable in relation to those services. As a rule, salaries are considered reasonable if they are representative of an amount that would be paid to an arm's-length party for similar services — in other words, comparable to what you would pay an unrelated employee to do that job.

▶ *TAX TIP*

There are many advantages to paying reasonable wages to family members for actual services rendered. One is that salaries will be taxed in their hands and probably at rates lower than the top marginal rate. This arrangement will also allow them to make their own RRSP and CPP contributions.

9. EMPLOYMENT INSURANCE AND FAMILY MEMBERS

Rules relating to withholding Employment Insurance premiums (better known as Unemployment Insurance prior to 1996) from salaries paid to spouses have changed several times over the last few years. Most recently, changes have been brought in that can have consequences for other family members as well. Essentially, you are not required to withhold Employment Insurance premiums from the salary of any employee who is related to you, unless it is reasonable to assume that a similar employment arrangement would have been negotiated with any other arm's-length person. In other words, if an individual not related to you would have been offered the same pay and work arrangements as those provided to your relative for the same services, you generally must withhold premiums from the salary paid to your relative.

▶ *TAX TIP*

If your spouse or other family members are currently employed by you, review the conditions surrounding their employment to determine if Employment Insurance premiums are required – you could be eligible for a refund.

10. CALCULATING DEPRECIATION

The cost of a capital asset is generally not deductible as an expense. However, you can depreciate certain business assets for tax purposes. In tax circles such depreciation is referred to as capital cost allowance (CCA).

Depreciable assets are grouped into classes according to their type and use. And Revenue Canada has come up with more than 40 different classes, each with its own rate of depreciation. Office equipment and furniture, for example, are depreciated at a rate of 20% per annum. General-purpose computers and systems software are depreciated at 30%, as are automobiles **(see article 16)**. Any building acquired after 1987 is usually depreciated at 4%. Most classes of assets are depreciated on a declining-balance basis.

How to calculate

The amount of depreciation you may claim for a year is arrived at by multiplying the remaining balance in the asset class by the percentage rate for that specific class. The remaining balance, referred to as the undepreciated capital cost (UCC), is calculated on a continuous basis.

The general rule is that property may be depreciated for tax purposes at the earlier of the time it is used to earn income or in the second taxation year following the year of acquisition.

Each year (subject to the available-for-use rules — see below), you add the cost of assets acquired in the year to the previous year's closing balance. If there have been any dispositions, you subtract the sale proceeds, up to the original cost of the disposed assets.

The half-year rule

Most depreciable assets are subject to a rule that reduces the maximum depreciation claim in the year of purchase to one-half of the normal amount. This "half-year" rule does not apply to the acquisition of certain capital property, such as tools costing less than $200 each. You can write them off 100% in the year of purchase.

EXAMPLE

Sample depreciation

Assume that you purchase a computer system in June 1998, for use in your consulting business. Total cost is $20,000. The computer would be placed in Class 10 and depreciated at a rate of 30% per year subject to the half-year rule. The CCA claim in 1998 and following years would be as follows:

Year	Opening UCC	CCA (30%)	Closing UCC
1998	20,000	3,000*	17,000
1999	17,000	5,100	11,900
2000	11,900	3,570	8,330
—			

*CCA rate for 1998 is 15% (30% x 1/2) – half-year rule applied in year of purchase.

In computing the 1998 business income for the consulting business referred to in this example, you may claim any amount up to $3,000 in respect of CCA. If you choose to claim a lesser amount, say $2,000, the difference is added to the UCC at the end of the year.

Available-for-use rules

For assets acquired after December 31, 1989, the available-for-use rules apply. These rules determine the taxation year in which an amount can first be claimed for depreciation and whether or not the half-year rule will apply. Rules with respect to the acquisition, construction and/or renovation of a building are especially complex — best to run this by your tax adviser before making a decision.

The maximum depreciation claim may also be reduced for short taxation years. Generally, if the fiscal period of your business is less than 12 months, the depreciation you are entitled to claim is prorated based on the number of days in your fiscal period. Also you should take note that a few classes of assets are excluded from this rule. Again, it's best to let your tax adviser assess whether it's applicable.

▶ *TAX TIP*

You should be aware that the rate for a particular class of assets represents the maximum rate that can be applied to the undepreciated capital cost of that class. You do not have to claim the maximum depreciation in any particular year. For example, if your business is in a loss position, you may decide that it is not beneficial to claim depreciation at that particular time.

Special rules and restrictions

Some depreciation restrictions apply to rental property **(see articles 88 and 90)** and to depreciation claims arising from certain "tax shelters" where the investor is not active in the day-to-day operation of the business. Depreciation claims by taxpayers who are in the leasing business are also subject to certain rules. To further complicate things, the rules do not apply to all leasing properties. Your tax adviser is in the best position to determine if you are affected by these rules.

In some circumstances, the CCA system does not adequately reflect variations in depreciation actually experienced due to rapid technological change. It is not uncommon at all for some equipment to become obsolete before being fully depreciated for income tax purposes. As a result, a special rule was introduced that allows you to elect to place certain types of capital property acquired after April 26, 1993, into a separate CCA class.

The CCA rate will not change in the separate class. However, if you sell or dispose of the property before five years, you can claim a terminal loss to the extent the UCC of the asset exceeds proceeds from the sale. Eligible property includes the following where each has a cost of $1,000 or more: general-purpose electronic data processing equipment, computer software, photocopiers and certain communications equipment.

> ▶ **TAX TIP**
> Eligible property may only be set up in a separate class if you make an election (by way of letter), and attach it to the return for the year the property is acquired.

11. YEAR 2000 EXPENDITURES

While millions of people around the world are anxiously anticipating the celebrations as the new millennium arrives, many businesses are just as anxiously keeping their eyes on something else. Their concern is the anticipated costs for adapting their computer systems to ensure proper operation when the year 2000 logs in.

Unless changes are made, many computers in use today will assume that the year 1900 has been reached when the date January 1, 2000, is input into a program. The resulting confusion and costly systems crashes can well be imagined.

To alleviate some of the cost expected in dealing with the situation, the Department of Finance recently announced measures to provide tax relief for small- and medium-sized businesses. Revenue Canada has provided general guidance on the tax treatment for these expenditures.

The facts surrounding each case will determine whether the expenditure should be expensed or treated as a capital asset. A capital asset cost is not deductible as an expense, but is eligible for the capital cost allowance (CCA) **(see article 10)**. What will be considered in making the determination is whether the expenditure was made with a view to creating an asset or an advantage of an enduring benefit.

EXAMPLE

Deductible or not

Suppose you incur costs to eliminate a year 2000 problem with an affected software program. If the costs cover restoring the software to its original condition, so that it performs the same applications but without the problem, for its originally assessed useful life, then the expenditure will normally be considered a deductible expense. However, if the expenditure also improves or enhances the software, it would usually be considered as the cost of a capital asset.

The government confirmed that expenditures on computer chips and firmware — software that is embedded in a computer chip — will be also be treated in a similar manner. This means that these expenditures will be fully deductible if they are incurred only to ensure functionality in the year 2000.

Expenditures for new software or other assets acquired to ensure that existing software is adapted for the year 2000 will be considered as the cost of a capital asset.

Additional tax relief

For small- and medium-sized businesses tax relief will be provided in the form of accelerated CCA deductions. Essentially, the accelerated CCA will allow these businesses to deduct 100% of the eligible capital expenditures in the year incurred. Eligible expenditures include year 2000 compliant computer hardware and software that is acquired to replace non-compliant hardware and software originally acquired before 1998. But take note, only expenditures for hardware and software acquired from January 1, 1998, to June 30, 1999, will be eligible.

The maximum additional deduction available to a taxpayer or a partnership will be limited to $50,000. Also only unincorporated businesses and corporations not subject to the Large Corporations Tax will be eligible. As always, special rules will apply to corporate groups and partnerships that have corporate members.

To claim this special treatment, you must file an election with Revenue Canada — by way of a letter attached to your tax return — outlining the property acquired, its cost, date of acquisition and a description of the property being replaced.

A review of your computer systems should be a priority at this point to ensure that they are year 2000 compliant, and to prevent a possible catastrophic failure of your systems and the ensuing monetary loss. If you are uncertain about the appropriate tax treatment for year 2000 expenditures, contact your professional adviser.

12. THE HOME OFFICE

Many Canadians now work out of their homes, and if you are among that rapidly burgeoning population you are probably aware that you can deduct a portion of your home office expenses. But like everything else when it comes to taxation, there are specific rules by which you must abide.

Expenses must relate to work space that is either your principal place of business or used exclusively for the purpose of earning income from the business. For the second criterion to apply, the space must also be used on a regular and continuous basis for meeting clients, customers or patients. Space set aside for your business must be a room or rooms used exclusively for the business. Setting up a computer and a filing cabinet in a corner of the living room may not entitle you to claim home office expenses.

Home office expenses can only be deducted from the business carried on in the home and cannot be used to create a business loss. Eligible expenses that you cannot use in the year they are incurred can be carried forward to subsequent years and deducted from income generated by the business at that time.

EXAMPLE

Carrying forward

Suppose you started a business in 1998. It generates revenues in 1998 of $25,000, expenses other than home office expenses of $20,000. The portion of eligible home expenses attributable to your office space amount to $8,000. In 1998, you will be able to claim only $5,000 of the home office expenses (i.e., $25,000 - 20,000). The remaining $3,000 of home office expenses can be carried forward and claimed against income generated by the business, provided there is sufficient income to do so.

▶ *TAX TIPS*

Keep a well-organized file of all receipts and record of payments and go over them with your tax adviser to see if they are eligible deductions for your at-home business. You may be able to deduct a portion of your house expenses such as property taxes, insurance, electricity, heat and mortgage interest.

In general, it's not a good idea to claim depreciation on the portion of your home used for business purposes, as there may be tax implications if you ever sell your home. By not claiming depreciation, your entire house may be regarded as your principal residence—that way any gain realized on the eventual sale of your house may be tax-free.

The GST element

Again, as with income tax restrictions, GST input tax credits can only be claimed on home office expenses if your home work space is the principal place of business or used exclusively for the purpose of earning income from a business on a regular and continuous basis. Input tax credits claimed must represent a reasonable portion of the expense that can be attributed to the business activity. There is no restriction on the method used, but once an allocation method is decided upon, it must be used consistently throughout the particular year. However, it may be changed in the following year.

▶ **TAX TIP**

GST registrants can claim an input tax credit for GST paid on home office expenses even if they are not able to deduct them in the year because of the limitation on creating or increasing losses.

EXAMPLE

GST and home office costs

You are a GST registrant, and your only office is located in your home. You regularly meet with clients and conduct all your business from this location. The office space occupies about 20% of the total area of the house. As such, you are entitled to claim a deduction for 20% of the eligible home expenses incurred and input tax credits for 20% of the GST paid on those expenses. This is provided that the portion claimed is reasonable given the type of business and that specific part of your home is used solely for the business.

13. PAYING YOUR DUES

Many professionals and business people belong to recreational or dining clubs (e.g., golf and tennis clubs), because as the old saying goes "All work and no play..." However, annual dues payable to such organizations or facilities are not deductible expenses.

If you pay annual membership dues for an employee, the dues will not be regarded as a taxable benefit to the employee if it can be demonstrated that it is to your advantage for your employee to belong to the club. Similarly, amounts you pay for your employee's use of the facilities for promotional purposes would also not be regarded as a taxable benefit.

What's allowed and what's not

An employee's use of a recreational club for promotional purposes may not be viewed as a taxable benefit. At the same time, the Income Tax Act also specifically denies a deduction for such expenses. This was made clear by a 1993 Supreme Court decision *(Sie-Mac Pipeline Contractors Ltd.)* in Revenue Canada's favour whereby expenses incurred for entertaining and training clients at a lodge were disallowed.

Responding to the concerns raised by this case, Revenue Canada has since clarified its position. If property such as a lodge or golf course is used for business purposes, and those purposes do not include the entertainment or recreation of clients, suppliers, shareholders or employees, the department will allow a deduction for the related expenses. For instance, if you hold a business meeting at a golf club and the meeting does not involve playing golf or use of the other recreational facilities, the expenses incurred should be deductible. Again, this is provided the expenses are within reason.

As for meals and beverages consumed at such facilities, deductibility restrictions are the same as for meals and beverages consumed at other establishments **(see article 14)**. You must ensure that the costs are clearly itemized and, of course, incurred for the purpose of earning income.

▶ *TAX TIP*
   Keep accurate, timely and detailed documentation of the business purpose of such expenses to reduce the risk of being denied a legitimate deduction.

14. MEALS AND ENTERTAINMENT EXPENSES

Specific limitations are set on the amount you can deduct for meals and entertainment. Only 50% of business meals and entertainment expenses are deductible in most cases. This applies to everyone — individuals, corporations and partnerships.

On the links

Revenue Canada recently changed its administrative position regarding the deductibility of meal and beverage costs incurred at a golf club. Their position was that these expenses were not deductible. As of February 1998 these deductions will no longer be denied. Instead, these costs will be treated the same way as meals and beverages consumed at other establishments — subject to the 50% restriction. To administer this new position, Revenue Canada requires that meal and beverage expenses incurred at a golf club be clearly itemized. If your records show an all-inclusive charge that does not itemize specific costs, the deduction will not be available.

A few exceptions

The 50% rule does not apply in certain cases, such as the cost of providing meals consumed and recreation enjoyed by all the employees working at a particular place of business. Meals and entertainment expenses incurred for an event intended primarily to benefit a registered charity also escape the 50% limit. However, the cost of executive dining rooms and similar facilities is subject to the 50% limit. If you attend a convention at which meals and/or entertainment are provided, but the cost of the meals and entertainment is not noted separately, $50 per day will be subject to the 50% rule.

How GST fits in

GST paid on meals and entertainment expenses is subject to restriction — only 50% is creditable. You are allowed to claim all the GST paid on such expenses as they are incurred and then make an annual adjustment to add back half of the amount claimed in the year. Alternatively, you may claim only half the GST on such expenses as they are incurred, if this is easier for your accounting purposes.

▶ *TAX TIPS*
To simplify the 50% calculation, make a concerted effort to keep such costs segregated from other expenses.

Meal and entertainment expenses specifically identified on your invoice and billed directly back to your clients are not subject to the 50% limitation. Your client, however, would then be subject to this limitation.

15. WHICH PROVINCE GETS YOUR TAX?

Employment and investment income are taxed by the province in which you reside on December 31. This holds true even if the income was earned in another province. Business income, on the other hand, is taxed in the province where the business was conducted. If you carry on the same business in more than one province, there is quite an involved formula used to determine what portion of your business income is taxable and in which province. This is best left to your tax adviser's expertise.

EXAMPLE

Income allocation

Generally speaking, business income is allocated to each province based on the pro rata share of the total revenue earned and salaries and wages paid to employees in the province. Assume you have business income of $100,000. Your head office is in Ontario and there is a sales office in British Columbia. Each office had one employee earning $30,000 per year. Now, if $300,000 in revenue was generated in Ontario and $200,000 was earned in British Columbia, business income would be allocated as follows:

	Revenue ($)	Revenue (%)	Wages ($)	Wages (%)
Ontario	300,000	60	30,000	50
B.C.	200,000	40	30,000	50
Total	500,000	100	60,000	100

Therefore, the business income taxable in Ontario would be $55,000 [100,000 x (60% + 50%)/2] and $45,000 [100,000 x (40% + 50%)/2] would be taxable in British Columbia.

> ▶ *TAX TIP*
> Provincial tax is based on your province of residence at December 31. If you are moving/transferring to a province with a lower tax rate you should consider accelerating your departure to arrive before the end-of-year deadline. Conversely, if a move to a province with a higher tax rate is in your future, if at all possible postpone your relocation until after the year-end.

16. AUTOMOBILE EXPENSES

If you are entitled to claim automobile expenses, beware — rules governing these deductions are extremely complex and as such cannot be covered here in any great detail. They apply equally to corporations, proprietors and partnerships, as well as to employees who qualify to claim automobile expenses against their employment income.

Expenses must first be split into two categories — those subject to specific dollar limitations and those that are not. Depreciation, interest and leasing charges are subject to specific dollar restrictions. The amount you can claim with respect to these restricted expenses depends on when the vehicle was acquired. Here are the maximum amounts relating to when the vehicles were purchased:

	Depreciation Base	Monthly Interest
After August 1989 and before 1991	$24,000 (including PST)	$300
1991 to 1996	$24,000 (plus PST & GST)*	$300
During 1997	$25,000 (plus PST & GST)*	$250
After 1997	$26,000 (plus PST & GST)*	$250

*GST is not included in the depreciation base if it is refunded as an input tax credit

The maximum amounts for vehicle leases are as follows:

	Monthly lease payment
Leases entered into prior to 1997	$650 (plus PST & GST)
Leases entered into in 1997	$550 (plus PST & GST)
Leases entered into after 1997	$650 (plus PST & GST)

For unincorporated businesses, the total of the restricted and unrestricted expenses is then prorated between business and personal use based on the number of kilometres you have driven for each purpose. Expenses, such as parking, incurred entirely for business purposes can be claimed in full. Corporations do not have to prorate expenses between business and personal use. Expenses can be claimed in full, provided they are reasonable. However, the employee may have to report a taxable benefit for personal expenses paid by the company **(see article 112)**.

Recapture

Most vehicle purchases before June 17, 1987, were added to a depreciable pool of assets identified as Class 10. Now, if you dispose of your only Class 10 asset without replacing it, and the proceeds from the sale exceed the undepreciated balance in the class, you will have to report the excess amount as income. This amount is known as recapture.

EXAMPLE

Recapture liability
You acquire an automobile for $20,000 in 1996 and sell it in 1998 for $14,000. The vehicle is used entirely for business purposes. If you claimed the maximum CCA in 1996 and 1997, the undepreciated amount at the beginning of 1998 would be $11,900 **(see example in Section 10)**. Therefore, you have to include $2,100 as recapture in income in 1998 (i.e., $14,000 - $11,900).

Since June 1987, passenger vehicles that cost more than a prescribed amount (currently $26,000, net of GST and PST) are included in a separate depreciable class identified as Class 10.1. Only the first $26,000 (plus GST and PST on $26,000) can be depreciated for tax purposes. However, there is no recapture when such a vehicle is disposed of, even if proceeds from the sale exceed the undepreciated balance in the class. Also note that one-half of the regular CCA can be claimed in the year of disposition.

If you as a proprietor or partner use your vehicle less than 100% for business purposes, the eligible depreciation claim for the year is generally determined by the percentage of business use.

▶ **TAX TIP**
Unless your vehicle is used 100% for business (or employment) purposes, you should keep detailed records regarding its use for business and personal operation. These records must be accurately maintained to support the percentage you claim for business use if Revenue Canada ever calls it into question.

17. GST AND PASSENGER VEHICLES

The complexity of the automobile rules is taken a step further by the GST factor. The input tax credit on passenger vehicles is limited to the tax on $26,000, excluding PST and GST. Outside of the provinces with a harmonized sales tax, the maximum tax that can be claimed as a credit is $1,820. In Nova Scotia, New Brunswick and Newfoundland and Labrador, where a harmonized tax has been established, the maximum tax credit available is $3,900.

Special rules apply to GST registered individuals and partnerships where the vehicle is not used more than 90% in a commercial activity. Generally, GST is recovered based on annual deductible capital cost allowance claims **(see article 16).**

EXAMPLE

GST and your auto

A GST-registered individual purchases an automobile for $16,000, including GST. He uses the vehicle 60% in commercial activities and 40% for personal use, based upon kilometres driven in the year. The maximum capital cost allowance the individual may claim on the automobile in the year of purchase is $1,440 ($\frac{1}{2}$ x 30% x $16,000 x 60%).

Because the individual uses the automobile less than 90% in commercial activities, for GST purposes, the individual may claim an input tax credit of $94 (7/107 x $1,440), assuming the maximum capital cost allowance is claimed.

Sales and trade-ins

And if all that is not enough, the GST must also be considered if a vehicle is sold or traded in. If a GST registrant uses a passenger vehicle primarily (more than 50%) in a commercial activity, the sale or trade-in of the vehicle is taxable. Any GST not previously recovered on the vehicle because of the cost limitation can then be claimed as an input tax credit. Individuals and partnerships do not collect tax on the sale or trade-in unless it is used exclusively in a commercial activity.

Taxable benefits

An employee or shareholder provided with a vehicle for personal use is deemed to be receiving a taxable benefit **(see article 112)**. If the employer or corporation is a GST registrant, the benefit is deemed to be a taxable supply and GST must be remitted on the benefit amount. Employers must remit the tax on their GST return that covers the last day of February each year — in other words, for the period that includes the due date for filing T4 slips for the relevant year. Corporations benefiting shareholders, on the other hand, report the tax on the GST return for the last day of the taxation year.

How much do you owe?

After 1995 the GST to be remitted is calculated by formula and, surprisingly, not directly tied to the actual GST paid. The formula varies with the nature of the benefit and whether the employee or shareholder being taxed on the benefit works or lives in a participating province. The remittance is calculated as follows:

	Stand-by charge	Operating cost benefit
Outside participating provinces	6/106ths	5.0%
Participating provinces		
1998 and later	14/114ths	11.0%

▶ TAX TIP

If personal use of the automobile is high and the employee or shareholder incurs most, but not all, of the operating costs, the taxable operating cost benefit and related GST remittance may be higher than the portion of actual operating costs paid by the employer. It's not a bad idea from time to time to review employment arrangements to determine if any changes should be made.

EXAMPLE

Splitting costs

An automobile is made available to an employee in a non-participating province, and that individual drives 14,000 personal kilometres and only 6,000 business kilometres in the year. The employer pays only $500 of the operating costs and the employee pays the remainder. An operating cost benefit of $1,960 (14¢ per personal kilometre) must be reported and the employer must remit $98 of GST on the benefit.

---

18. CONVENTION EXPENSES

Under current rules, if you are carrying on a business or practising a profession, you may deduct expenses that come with attending conventions. Deductions are allowed for attendance at two conventions a year. These conventions must relate to your business and be held within the territory in which the sponsoring organization conducts its affairs. You can deduct 50% of the actual cost of meals and entertainment incurred at conventions **(see article 14)**. If these items are not segregated from the rest of the costs, a deemed cost of $50 per day is attributed, which is then subject to the 50% provision.

Expenses must be reasonable and you should be in a position to prove your attendance and to support your expenses with vouchers.

▶ TAX TIP

When your spouse attends a convention with you, the associated cost is usually seen as a personal non-deductible expense. But, if there are good business reasons for your spouse to accompany you, these expenses may also be deductible.

19. DEDUCTION OF HEALTH/DENTAL INSURANCE PREMIUMS

The 1998 federal budget proposed to allow self-employed individuals to deduct, within limits, premiums paid for private health services plan coverage against their business income, provided certain conditions are met.

In order for the premiums to be deductible, individuals must be actively engaged either alone or as a partner in their businesses, and self-employment must be their primary source of income in the current year, or their income from other sources must not exceed $10,000.

In addition, equivalent coverage must be extended to all permanent full-time arm's-length employees. Where a deduction is claimed, no amount paid for coverage will be eligible for the medical expense tax credit **(see article 61)**. This is effective for fiscal periods commencing after 1997.

20. QUALIFIED SCIENTIFIC RESEARCH EXPENDITURES

Writeoffs and tax credits above and beyond your usual business deductions are possible if you conduct scientific research that relates to your business. Research and development (R&D) consists of pure research, applied research and experimental development. The first two items relating to research activities do not usually cause a problem. The development side of the coin does. Part of the problem is that it is often difficult to define what constitutes development. It is also equally difficult to distinguish exactly when development ceases and production begins. And production does not qualify as research and development. Your accountant will be able to assess if your R&D qualifies, or what you may have to do to ensure your R&D activities are recognized by Revenue Canada.

What can you deduct?

Generally, all qualifying research expenditures of a current nature may be deducted in full in the year they are incurred. However, a current year deduction will not be permitted for amounts accrued in respect of remuneration if that remuneration is not paid within 180 days of the end of the taxation year. Subject to the available-for-use rules **(see article 10)**, equipment purchased to be used solely for qualifying research in Canada may also be written off in the year it is acquired. As a rule, expenditures incurred to acquire or rent a building do not qualify as scientific research expenditures.

▶ *TAX TIP*
You don't have to claim the full amount of eligible R&D expenses in the year in which they were incurred. It may make better business sense to carry forward and deduct the amounts in any subsequent year. This is provided you are carrying on the business to which the research relates in the year you

make the claim. For example, in some years it may be advantageous not to deduct an amount where a deduction will increase a non-capital loss, the carry-forward of which will expire in seven years. By the same token, it may be advantageous to carry forward the deduction to a year in which the deduction could be claimed against a higher marginal tax rate.

Claiming R&D

To claim special treatment for scientific research expenditures, you must complete form T661. This requires you to provide a breakdown of the expenditures made, as well as details of the types of projects undertaken, such as the scientific or technological content, advancements made and uncertainties pursued. It is vital that project descriptions are complete. Failure to describe the projects properly could result in a rejection of the claim or, at best, it could significantly delay processing.

Beginning with taxation years after 1995, outlays will be disqualified as research and development expenditures unless form T661 is filed within 12 months of the filing due date for the taxation year. In other words, if a corporation with a December 31 year-end incurs R&D expenditures, form T661 (for the 1998 taxation year) must be filed by June 30, 2000. That's because the filing due date of the corporate income tax return is June 30, 1999, six months from the December 31, 1998, year-end.

Not all the news from the tax department means more complications for you. It was recently announced that a new simplified application form will be introduced to streamline the paperwork required for small businesses, but only certain corporations will be eligible to use this simplified form. Your tax adviser will have further information on eligibility.

Investment tax credit

Both current and capital expenditures on scientific research may qualify for the business investment tax credit (ITC) **(see article 21)**. The 20% or 35% rate of credit for qualifying R&D expenditures varies according to the status of the claimant, and the claimant's taxable income and taxable capital **(see article 5)** for the prior year.

A Canadian-controlled private corporation (CCPC) is eligible for the 35% tax credit rate on up to $2 million of qualifying R&D expenditures in the year. This is provided taxable income did not exceed $200,000 and taxable capital did not exceed $10 million in the preceding year. A CCPC whose taxable income for the preceding year was between $200,000 and $400,000 or whose taxable capital was between $10 million and $15 million will also be eligible for the 35% rate. However the $2-million limit on qualifying expenses will be reduced.

When determining eligibility for this rate of credit, the taxable income and taxable capital includes those of the corporation and all associated corporations. Qualifying expenditures not eligible for the 35% rate will be eligible for the 20% rate.

▶ TAX TIPS

In order to qualify for an ITC, you must make sure all current R&D expenditures are paid within 180 days of the year-end.

In the case of equipment that is only used partially for R&D, the cost may not be written off as an eligible R&D expenditure. Still, if the equipment is used primarily (more than 50%) for R&D, the cost may be eligible for a reduced ITC.

Overhead expenses

Much of the Income Tax Act can be cited as confounding, but one area that has always caused confusion is in the determination of eligible R&D overhead expenses. You have the option of calculating eligible overhead expenses using a simple formula based on wages and salaries. The amount arrived at in this manner is called the "proxy amount." In general, this amount is calculated as 65% of the portion of salaries or wages of employees directly engaged in R&D in Canada.

The proxy amount is added to the expenses eligible for an ITC. Even so, it does not increase the amount of R&D expenditures available for deduction. Again, there are special rules that limit the amount of salary to be used in the calculation. These apply if that salary has been paid to an employee who does not deal at arm's length with the taxpayer, or to an employee who owns or is related to someone who owns 10% or more of the shares of the employer corporation.

▶ *TAX TIP*

The use of the "proxy amount" is elective and if you choose to use this method for a particular year, the election to Revenue Canada must be made at the time form T661 is first filed for that year.

Provincial incentives

A number of investment tax credits and other tax incentives for R&D are offered by several of the provinces. The R&D must be carried out in the province that grants these tax breaks. And while these credits may reduce the amount of expenditures eligible for federal ITCs, they generally help reduce the overall cost of R&D.

▶ *TAX TIP*

Not incorporated? Here's another reason to mull it over. If you are carrying on a business and conduct scientific research that relates to that business, you should consider incorporating as your business can benefit from the enhanced ITCs and provincial incentives, which are available only to corporations. Once more, the rules involved in claiming scientific R&D expenditures and related investment tax credits are extremely complex. Consult with your tax adviser to ensure you get the maximum benefit from these tax incentives.

21. BUSINESS INVESTMENT TAX CREDIT

Investment tax credits (ITCs) reduce federal taxes and can, in some cases, create cash refunds to qualifying corporations and individuals. Over the years though, the ITC system has been gradually scaled back. ITCs are now available only on qualified scientific R&D projects. They are also available on qualifying property acquired for use in certain regions of the country to stimulate economic development, notably the Atlantic provinces and the Gaspé region of Québec.

Using unused credits

Now that you've acquired the credits, there are a few ways to employ them. If those earned in a current year exceed federal taxes payable, you may be able to use the excess to generate a refund. Or if it is to your advantage, you can carry unused credits back up to three years or forward up to ten years.

Currently, this refundable system is available only to individuals and certain CCPCs. In general, the refundable portion is equal to 40% of the unused credits. However, R&D ITCs earned at the 35% rate are eligible for a 100% refund if the ITC relates to current R&D expenditures.

ITCs either reduce the tax cost of the related asset or are included in income in the year following the year the credit is claimed.

New filing dates

As of February 18, 1997, a completed form T2038 — giving details of the qualifying cost or expense — must be filed within 12 months of the due date of the return for the taxation year in which the ITC arises. This filing deadline for all ITCs is similar to the filing deadline for scientific R&D expenditures. Later in 1998, the T2038 form may be replaced with a new one, the T2S(31). Your tax adviser can update you on that as well as ascertain whether you qualify for the investment tax credit.

22. ASSOCIATED COMPANY RULES

To prevent taxpayers from creating more than one corporation to enjoy the benefits of the small business deduction, Revenue Canada requires that the annual limit of $200,000 be shared among associated companies. The application of the concept of associated companies is a common one in the Income Tax Act, and the definition, like that of many other tax rules, is quite complex. The simplest cases are those where companies are under common control or one is controlled by the other.

EXAMPLE

ABCs of association

Company A controls Company B, so Company A and Company B are associated with each other. If Company A also controls Company C, then each of companies A, B and C are associated with each other.

Control of a company is not just measured by ownership of the voting shares. In addition to the traditional voting control test, "control" is recognized if a person, or group of persons, owns more than 50% of the fair market value of all of the issued shares, or more than 50% of the corporation's common equity shares. To make things more exciting, control can also arise when a person, or group of persons, has any direct or indirect influence that, if exercised, would result in control "in fact" of the corporation.

Sorting out ownership

Who owns the shares? Revenue Canada looks through a corporation to deem the ownership in the hands of the shareholders of a corporation — for example, if you own 60% of one company, which in turn owns 30% of another company, you are regarded as owning 18% (60% of 30%) of the company that is owned by your company.

Shares owned by children under age 18 are generally considered to be owned by the parent. In addition to all the technical rules governing association, a general rule is still on the books whereby companies are considered to be associated if one of the main reasons for their separate existence is to save tax.

The concept of control is quite far reaching, yet it is possible for related persons to invest in each other's companies and still remain non-associated. To accomplish that, the cross-ownership limit of less than 25% cannot be exceeded. A case in point — if you own 100% of Company A and 20% of Company B with the other 80% owned by your spouse, Company A and Company B will not automatically be associated. Also, certain types of shares known as shares of a "specified class" are specifically excluded in determining control and cross-ownership.

> ▶ *TAX TIP*
>
> Have you an interest in one or more companies that are related to each other or to other companies? If so, have your tax adviser review the corporate structure to see whether you are deemed to be associated and if there are ways to prevent association.

23. VALUATION OF INVENTORY

There are two methods generally used to establish value of business inventory for tax purposes. All items may be valued at fair market value (as at the end of the particular year), or each item may be valued at whatever is the lower — its cost or its fair market value.

Late in 1995, as a result of the Supreme Court of Canada's decision in the case of *Friesen v. The Queen*, the government announced changes to the inventory valuation rules as they apply to property held as an "adventure or concern in the nature of trade." This designation usually refers to a one-time transaction often conducted by an individual. For taxation years ending after December 20, 1995, the general rule above will continue to apply to most businesses. However, property held as inventory of an adventure in the nature of trade must be valued at the cost at which the taxpayer acquired it, although certain additions to this cost are allowable. What this change does is deny the recognition of a loss on the property until the property is disposed of. A common example of a situation in which this may apply is if you hold land on the speculation that it can be sold at a profit without further development.

24. INSTALMENT SALES

If selling property to your customers on an instalment-sale basis is part of your business, you should be aware of tax rules relating to instalment sales. To qualify for a tax deferral, the instalment sale must be for a period of more than two full years. However, if the property sold was land, the instalment sale need only be for a period that ends after the closing of the fiscal period in which the sale was made.

How much can you defer?

You can spread the profit over a maximum of four years including the year of sale, if you qualify. The amount you can defer is the pro rata portion of your profit. That is based on the ratio of the amount not due at each year-end, to the total sales price. In the third fiscal year following the sale, you must include all of the remaining untaxed profit in income, even if there is still an amount not due until a subsequent year.

EXAMPLE

Deferring tax

An airplane manufacturer sells a number of planes to a customer on March 31, 1998, for $1,200,000 and realizes a gross profit of $300,000 on the sale. Terms of sale require $400,000 to be paid on delivery and another $400,000 to be paid on June 30, 1999, and June 30, 2000. Assuming a December 31 year-end, the amount of profit available for the deferral in each year is calculated as follows:

1998:	$(800,000 / \$1,200,000) \times \$300,000 =$	$200,000
1999:	$(\$400,000 / \$1,200,000) \times \$300,000 =$	$100,000
2000:	$(\$0 / \$1,200,000) \times \$300,000 =$ $	0

As a result of the deferral, the gross profit of $300,000 will be included in income as follows:

1998:	$100,000
1999:	$100,000
2000:	$100,000

A different set of rules applies to instalment sales of property taxed as capital gains **(see article 95).**

---

25. OPERATING LOSSES AND PRIOR YEARS' TAXES

If you carried on a business as a proprietor or partner in 1998 and incurred an operating loss, you can apply the loss against other sources of income, such as investment income, capital gains and employment income.

How it works

Any loss realized in a year must be deducted in full against your other sources of income. As a result, you may find that you are unable to claim some or all of your non-refundable tax credits such as personal amounts and medical expenses. To that end you should check with your tax adviser to assess whether other family members can obtain the maximum benefit from these lost credits.

Should your operating loss exceed your other sources of income too, the excess may be carried back three years or forward up to seven years. To carry the loss back, you must file form T1A with your return for the year in which the loss arises. Technically, you are supposed to make the request by the filing deadline for the year the loss arises. However, Revenue Canada tends to use its discretion as long as the prior year is still open to reassessment. You are free to choose the year to which you want to apply the loss. One scenario is if you expect your marginal rate of tax to increase in the future, you may decide to carry the loss forward rather than back to a prior year.

▶ *TAX TIP*

When carrying a loss back to a prior year, you have the option of using only a portion of your loss. It is generally more effective to claim non-refundable tax credits, most of which have no carryover, and apply the remaining unusable loss to another year.

26. AMORTIZATION AND SALE OF GOODWILL

Taxpayers who have purchased goodwill related to a business are permitted to depreciate or amortize three-quarters of the cost on a declining-balance basis at the rate of 7%. When goodwill (the intangible value of a business such as a recognized name and reputation) is sold, three-quarters of the proceeds are credited to the unamortized pool at the time of sale and, if the balance of the pool becomes negative, the negative balance is taxed as business income.

Based on the timing of prior amortization claims, certain additional adjustments may have to be made to this negative balance. If you have not incurred any costs in acquiring goodwill, three-quarters of the sale proceeds will be included in business income.

Capital gains vs. income

Under the current rule you are required to report the negative balance of the pool as business income. However, if a sale took place in a fiscal period that ended prior to February 23, 1994, the portion of the negative balance that corresponded to amounts previously claimed as amortization was included in income as business income and the remainder was a taxable capital gain. This taxable capital gain was eligible for the capital gains deduction **(see article 92)**.

▶ *TAX TIP*

Certain expenditures incurred in relation to a business may not be deductible from income since they are capital in nature but still not eligible for CCA treatment **(see article 10)**. That being the case, you should review these items with your tax adviser to determine if any of the expenditures would qualify for amortization, as discussed above.

27. CANADA PENSION PLAN CONTRIBUTIONS

Did you earn income from a business as a proprietor or partner in 1998? Then you may be liable for contributions under the Canada Pension Plan (CPP). If you did not earn any employment income in the year, your contribution for 1998 is 6.4% of the difference between your net business income and a $3,500 standard exemption, subject to a maximum contribution of $2,137.60.

If you earned employment income, the amount of CPP premiums that have been withheld from this income is a factor in determining the amount you have to pay. Suppose your 1998 net business income was $30,000, your CPP contribution for 1998 would be $1,696 [6.4% x ($30,000 - $3,500)]. However, if you also had $10,000 in employment income, your required CPP contributions in respect of your business income would be adjusted to take into account two factors. One, your total earnings exceed the maximum pensionable earnings ($36,900); and two, the basic exemption of $3,500 may already have been taken on your employment income. Let's assume you and your employer have already contributed $416 [6.4% x ($10,000 - $3,500)] in respect of your employment income; your CPP contribution in respect of your business income would be $1,722 {[(36,900 - $3,500) x 6.4%]- $416}.

Contributions commence the month after you reach the age of 18 and can be made until the age of 70. CPP contributions generate a nonrefundable tax credit on your individual tax return. This tax credit equals 17% of the required contributions (approximately 26% after taking into account provincial tax rates).

28. CORPORATE LOSSES AND CHANGE OF CONTROL

When you acquire control of a corporation, a number of rules restrict your ability to carry forward losses that were incurred before your takeover. At the same time, some of these rules require certain adjustments be made to various accounts for income tax purposes. The intent is to crystallize any losses inherent in the corporation's assets.

Claiming losses

Claiming non-capital (operating) losses in any period after the change of control requires the business that generated the losses to carry on throughout the year with a reasonable expectation of profit. In addition, these losses may only be claimed to the extent of the income generated from that business or a similar business. Similar rules apply on the carry-forward of unused R&D expenses and business investment tax credits. Any unused net capital losses at the time of the change in control may not be used after that point.

> ▶ *TAX TIP*
> There are some tax-planning techniques available to utilize operating losses
> that might otherwise be forfeited in the carry-forward period. If you are con-
> sidering acquiring control of a corporation in an effort to utilize its tax loss-
> es, R&D expenses **(see article 20)** or ITCs **(see article 21)**, make sure you
> are fully aware of the rules as they apply to your situation before you make
> your purchase.

29. DEDUCTION OF LIFE INSURANCE PREMIUMS

If you are required to purchase life insurance as part of the package
when borrowing money for business purposes, you can deduct the cost
of the premiums, provided certain tests are met. In order for a deduction to be claimed, the policy must be assigned to the lender as security for the loan and the lender must require this assignment. In addition,
the lender's principal business must be the lending of money, and the
interest payable on the loan must be deductible for income tax purposes (or would be deductible except in the case of special overriding rules).

The amount that can be claimed is restricted to the net cost of pure
insurance. The portion of the premium that is deductible could be
reduced if the balance of the loan outstanding is less than the amount
of insurance coverage.

Since 1995, life insurance premiums are not deductible for alternative minimum tax (AMT) purposes **(see article 110)**.

30. SHAREHOLDER AGREEMENTS

If your corporation has more than one shareholder, a shareholders'
agreement should be drawn up to establish the ongoing rights and
responsibilities of the shareholders in the ownership and administration
of the company.

In the event of death...

One of the more important aspects of the shareholders' agreement is
that it should specify what should happen in the event of the death or
disability of one of the shareholders. Not only will this provide for a
smooth transition of the business, but such agreements generally establish a purchaser for the shares of the deceased, a formula for determining the purchase price and a method for funding the purchase. By
arranging proper tax planning, the buy-out can be orchestrated to min-

imize a drain on cash flow for the company and survivors. A sound arrangement can also minimize or defer the tax liability of the estate.

The most efficient means of funding a buy-sell agreement or share repurchase on the death of a shareholder is generally though life insurance. However, the use of corporate-owned life insurance to fund a share repurchase may no longer be an effective tax strategy. It is highly advisable to arrange with your tax adviser to develop a plan that is appropriate to your situation.

▶ *TAX TIP*
Recently, the government enacted changes that may significantly alter the tax implications where life insurance proceeds are used to fund a share repurchase. One of the things that should be included at the top of your agenda is to undertake a review of your shareholders' agreement. That way you can ensure your objectives are met in the most tax-effective manner.

31. TRANSFER PRICING

A transfer price is a price charged between related parties involved in international transactions — for example, where a Canadian resident buys goods and services from or sells to a related non-resident corporation. The government's concern centres on ensuring that the price charged is equal to the amount that would be agreed upon by parties dealing at arm's length. If it is not, taxable profits may be shifted from one jurisdiction to another.

Recent legislation on transfer pricing mirrors new laws recently put in place in other industrialized countries such as the United States, the United Kingdom and Australia. It requires Canadian taxpayers to adopt the arm's-length principle in setting transfer prices for transactions with related non-resident persons and to document the basis of the transfer pricing.

The arm's-length principle has always been required in transactions with related persons, but the new, more specific requirement applies for tax years commencing after 1997. Documentation standards are applicable for tax years commencing after 1998 and stipulate that the documentation for a particular tax year be completed by the due date for filing that year's tax return. Failure to complete the documentation can result in a penalty of 10% of the transfer pricing adjustment. The penalty can apply even though no additional tax arises as a result of the transfer pricing adjustment.

▶ *TAX TIP*

If you have transactions with related non-resident persons, have your tax adviser review your transfer pricing polices as well as related documentation to determine whether they comply with the new legislation.

32. THE GOODS ON THE GST

The 7% GST is a consumption tax on most goods and services provided in Canada. Unlike provincial sales taxes that are imposed only at the time of a sale to a consumer, the GST is a multi-level tax collected every time a taxable good or service is provided. Businesses that charge GST on their revenues can recover GST paid by claiming an "input tax credit," so that they bear no net tax.

As of April 1, 1997, Newfoundland and Labrador, New Brunswick and Nova Scotia repealed their respective provincial sales taxes and implemented the Harmonized Sales Tax (HST). It operates in the same manner and is applicable to the same base of goods and services as the GST. However, it is applied at a rate of 15%.

Supplies of goods or services are taxed in three ways. Most goods and services are rated as 7%-taxable supplies and attract tax at 7% outside the HST-participating provinces and 15% in the provinces using the HST. You don't have to keep track of how much tax is collected at 7% or 15%. All tax collected is to be remitted. Any GST-registered business that makes only 7%- or 15%-taxable supplies recovers all the GST it pays as an input tax credit. Again, it does not matter whether the tax is paid at 7% or 15%.

Tax is not collected on zero-rated supplies, but full input tax credits are claimed for the GST paid on related inputs. Zero-rated supplies include most basic foods, agricultural products, prescription drugs, medical devices and goods and services that are exported.

Exempt supplies are not subject to GST, but a business making them is not entitled to claim an input tax credit for the GST on related costs. In effect, a business making exempt supplies bears the cost of the GST and must factor it into the price of the goods and services sold. Long-term residential rents, health care services and financial services are the most common types of exempt supplies.

33. GST REGISTRATION, COLLECTION AND REMITTANCE

Unless a business has $30,000 or more in annual taxable sales, it is not required to register and collect tax. But be aware, revenues of associated entities are included in measuring annual taxable sales. Businesses not required to register are called "small suppliers." Such businesses can elect to register and collect tax as this enables them to claim input tax credits for any GST they pay on purchases **(see article 34)**. Generally this is advisable if the recipient of the supply is also a GST registrant.

Separate thresholds are used to determine whether charities and public sector bodies are required to register.

New businesses

Starting a new business venture? Then it is generally a good idea to register for GST as soon as possible. Early registration ensures that GST paid on costs incurred is recoverable, since any GST paid prior to registration can generally be recovered only on the purchase of inventory, capital property and prepaid services.

When to report

Every business has a GST reporting period based on its revenue. Most businesses are required to report quarterly. However, large businesses (over $6,000,000 in annual taxable supplies) must report monthly, while small businesses (under $500,000 in annual taxable supplies) may elect to report on an annual basis. New GST registrants with annual taxable supplies of under $500,000 are automatically assigned an annual reporting period, unless they choose to file more frequently.

> **▶ *TAX TIP***
> You can elect to report more frequently than required. This is advisable if you are generally in a net refund position, as businesses that sell a large percentage of zero-rated goods often are.

34. INPUT TAX CREDITS

If you have paid GST on goods and services used in making 7%-taxable, 15%-taxable and zero-rated supplies, you can claim input tax credits. To ensure that your claim will be allowed, you must have supporting documentation in your records in case your claim is ever challenged. You should thoroughly go over the detailed rules that govern the content of this supporting documentation, ensuring that you have complied with each stipulation. GST audit problems often arise through deficient documentation, even if the deficiency is minor.

If input tax credits claimed in a reporting period exceed the GST owing, the excess is refunded to the business.

Shorter time frame for some claims

There have been changes in the GST that affect registrants who are listed financial institutions, or whose taxable supplies for the preceding two years (including the supplies of associated businesses) exceed $6,000,000. These businesses now have only two years, as opposed to four years formerly, to claim input tax credits.

Revenue Canada, on the other hand, still has four years to audit a GST return. Therefore it is essential that such large businesses ensure their systems accurately and completely capture and claim all GST paid. Generally, businesses with 90% of their supplies being taxable supplies in either of the two immediately preceding fiscal years are excluded from the two-year restriction, as are charities. These registrants and all other registrants maintain the ability to claim input tax credits for a period of four years.

For businesses that make both taxable and exempt supplies, the GST paid on purchases must be allocated between the two types of supplies. Any reasonable method of allocation is acceptable, though it is not necessary to use the same method from year to year. The allocation of input tax credits allows you some scope for planning.

EXAMPLE
GST allocation

A GST registrant involved in both taxable and exempt activities incurs GST of $3,200 in respect to its occupancy costs. If 70% of the total floor space is used in commercial activities based upon the square footage, the registrant may choose to use this allocation method and claim $2,240 (70% x $3,200) as an input tax credit. Alternatively, the registrant may choose to base the allocation on the number of employees working in each particular activity.

▶TAX TIP

A business that must allocate the GST paid on purchases of both taxable and exempt supplies for purposes of claiming input tax credits should review its allocation method each year. Due to inherent changes in business activity, it may be advantageous to change the method used to allocate GST paid, as it may result in a higher recoverable percentage.

35. GST AND REAL PROPERTY SALES

As a general rule, real property sales are taxable, even when the vendor is a small supplier. In such cases, the vendor must collect and remit the GST. Major exemptions are the sale of used residential property and the sale of real property by an individual who is not engaged in a business. However, if the property has been subdivided into more than two parts, even an individual must charge GST when the property is sold.

GST is generally not collected on sales to a GST registrant. A business selling real property should ensure that the purchaser is a GST registrant before concluding that no GST will be collected on the sale. That is not to say that GST is not payable by the purchaser. If the property is not used in making taxable supplies, the purchaser is required to self-assess the tax. When real property is sold in a taxable transaction to a non-registrant, the vendor must collect the GST whether the vendor is registered or not.

▶TAX TIP

When a non-registrant sells real property, and the deal is subject to tax, the vendor can claim back any GST previously paid on the acquisition or improvement of the property that has not already been recovered. The GST is claimed back by filing a rebate form. If the vendor collects tax on the sale, the result is that the vendor sends Revenue Canada the net amount of the tax collected less the rebate amount. If the vendor does not collect tax on the sale (because the purchaser is registered), the rebate will be paid directly by Revenue Canada. The rebate application must be filed within two years of the date of sale.

36. GST AND BUYING AND SELLING A BUSINESS

A purchaser and vendor may be able to file a special election to avoid paying GST when business assets are sold. This election is usually available if the purchaser is acquiring ownership or use of all the property needed to carry on a business or a part of a business. The big difficulty arises as you try to determine if what is being sold qualifies for this election. Before signing the papers you should consult with your tax adviser about the advisability of seeking a ruling from Revenue Canada.

37. GST AUDITS

Although the GST has been making the lives of many Canadians a little more complicated since its inception in 1991, most of its technical provisions have yet to be tested in the courts. Furthermore, Revenue Canada's administrative policies continue to evolve as it gains more experience with the tax.

As with income tax audits, prevention is always better than a cure. A comprehensive review of systems and compliance can often resolve problems before being identified by the GST auditor. Many audit adjustments generate only interest and penalty payments — failure to collect tax on a sale will often be offset by an input tax credit to the recipient of the supply. In such cases, it is Revenue Canada's policy to allow the interest and penalties to be reduced to a penalty equal to 4% of the net amount of the tax owing on these transactions. A registrant does not have to apply for such relief. Revenue Canada's published policy is to provide the relief on assessment.

In This Section

Individuals

Individual taxpayers face a huge challenge with regard to tax implications and preparing to deal with them. Many tax pitfalls can be readily avoided through proper tax planning, just as there are many ways to reduce taxes by a thorough assessment of your circumstances.

This section addresses 50 of the most common areas that can affect your tax profile, both positively and negatively. It provides details on the various tax credits you can claim — credits that are often not used, as many Canadians are not aware that these tax relief measures are available to them.

Included, also, are a dozen or so items detailing the rules and the inherent versatility of one of Canada's best tax reduction tools — the Registered Retirement Savings Plan. As well, up-to-date information is presented on the recent changes to the rules and the improved attractiveness of Registered Education Saving Plans.

Other areas covered include the tax implications of owning more than one piece of real estate, how you can reduce your tax load by splitting income with family members, what's involved in becoming a Canadian resident, and by the same token what happens when you give up your Canadian residency. And last but certainly not least are details on one of the most overlooked but vitally important areas for you to consider — estate planning.

As with the other sections of this book, there are many tips to help you make smart choices as you draw up a tax strategy for your particular circumstances.

38. FILING A TAX RETURN

You are required to file an income tax return for a taxation year if you:

- have tax payable for that year
- sold or disposed of capital property in the year
- have to repay Old Age Security or Employment Insurance benefits
- want to apply for the Goods and Services Tax credit
- have self-employed earnings of $3,500 or more in the year and must make CPP contributions, even if your income is otherwise below taxable levels
- received a demand from Revenue Canada to file a return

In addition, you and your spouse are also required to file a return if you want to receive Child Tax Benefit payments.

▶ *TAX TIP*

Anyone, including minors, with "earned income" for RRSP purposes should consider filing an income tax return. RRSP contribution room, which may be used in subsequent years, will only accumulate if a tax return is filed **(see article 45)**.

39. YOUR RETURN IS DUE...

Your return must be mailed on or before April 30 of the following calendar year. In other words, your 1998 return will be due by April 30, 1999. This is particularly relevant if you owe the government a tax payment. Penalties on outstanding amounts begin to accumulate after that deadline. If you are owed a refund, it doesn't make any sense to wait until that date — much less past that date. File as soon as you have all your documentation; after all, the refund is your money and it's not doing you a lot of good sitting in the treasury.

Since the 1995 taxation year, if you or your spouse carry on a business (other than as a member of a limited partnership) during the year, you now have until June 15 of the following year to file your return.

EXAMPLE

Due dates

If you and your spouse were both employed full-time, and your spouse also had a part-time consulting business in 1998, each of you will have until June 15, 1999, to file your returns. However, any tax owing by you and your spouse must be paid by April 30, 1999.

▶ *TAX TIP*
Anticipating a refund? Then you should still file your return as early as possible. Interest on refunds will only be paid from June 15 or 45 days after you file your return, whichever is the latest date.

40. GST CREDIT

The GST credit is intended to offset GST paid by lower-income individuals and families during the year. It is paid in quarterly instalments following the due date for filing a return. Since a 1998 return is generally due by April 30, 1999, the quarterly payments will be scheduled for July and October 1999, and January and April 2000.

Subject to income restrictions, you are eligible to claim the credit. But you must, at the end of the year, be a resident of Canada and either 19 years of age or over, married or a parent. No credit can be claimed for a person who died during the year.

What's it worth?

The basic GST credit for an individual is $199. For families, the credit is $199 for yourself and $199 for your spouse (or other parent of your child). An eligible child will be credited with $105. If you are married and living with your spouse (or other parent of your child), only one of you may claim the credit for the family unit. It does not matter which of you claims the credit.

However, the total credit you may claim is reduced by 5% of your combined adjusted net incomes in excess of a specified threshold amount, which is $25,921 for 1998. Therefore, a married couple with two eligible children will qualify for the full credit of $608 if their combined family income is $25,921 or less. Their entitlement will decrease to zero once family income exceeds $38,081.

▶ *TAX TIP*
To apply for the GST credit you must file an income tax return. Individuals 19 years of age or older at the end of 1998 must apply for their own credits.

41. WHY BUY AN RRSP?

There are three compelling reasons for contributing to an RRSP — Registered Retirement Savings Plan. First, your contribution is tax deductible — the higher your marginal tax rate, the greater your tax savings. Second, the income generated by the plan is only taxed on withdrawal from the plan (usually when you are retired and possibly in a lower tax bracket). That means you can build up quite significant earnings inside your plan on a pre-tax basis. Finally, all or a portion of your annual eligible contribution may be contributed to a plan set up for your spouse.

Spousal plans
Setting up a spousal RRSP is advisable if you expect your spouse to be in a lower tax bracket than you on retirement. When funds are withdrawn from the spousal RRSP, they are taxed in your spouse's hands at his or her lower tax rate (this arrangement is subject to special rules to prevent abuse). What this succeeds in doing is reducing your family's total tax bill. This strategy also means that benefits such as the pension credit can be made available to both spouses, and you may reduce your exposure to the Old Age Security clawback **(see article 54)**.

The majority of Canadians do not focus on retirement planning early in their careers. Yet contributing to an RRSP as early as possible, even if it is not the maximum allowable amount, is a very powerful retirement planning strategy. Once you invest in an RRSP, you can earn income that compounds on a pre-tax basis. Depending on the type of investment products in your RRSP, this additional growth can often be far more substantial than the initial savings realized through the tax deduction.

> ▶ *TAX TIP*
> If you don't have an RRSP, don't worry, you're not alone. Despite the many benefits of an RRSP, many Canadians do not have one. However, you *should* fret about missing out on reducing your taxes and creating a substantial retirement nest egg that compounds tax-free. RRSPs are not at all hard to establish. Talk to a financial planner or your bank's financial services staff, who can set up an RRSP with a minimum of fuss or confusion. As for the type of RRSP to select, you should give consideration to a self-directed

plan – you don't really have to manage it, but it gives you much more flexibility in your financial and tax planning strategies **(see article 46)**.

42. HOW MUCH CAN YOU CONTRIBUTE?

Your maximum annual RRSP contribution is based on earned income in the previous year. Earned income includes salaries, business income, disability pensions (issued under the Canada and Quebec pension plans), taxable alimony/maintenance and rental income. Remember, too, your earned income is reduced by business losses, rental losses and deductible alimony/maintenance paid. Retiring allowances, investment income, capital gains or pension income are not classified as earned income.

Estimating your contribution limit

If you are not a member of a registered pension plan (RPP) or a deferred profit sharing plan (DPSP), you will be able to contribute 18% of your 1997 earned income to an RRSP in 1998 — up to a maximum of $13,500. That contribution must be made by March 1, 1999.

If you were not able to make the maximum contribution to your plan in any or all the years from 1991 to 1997, you can also make up the difference in 1998 **(see article 45)**. Your 1998 earned income will determine your 1999 contribution limit. The deadline for your 1999 RRSP will be February 29, 2000.

▶ *TAX TIPS*

Making the maximum RRSP contribution in 1998 will require earned income of at least $75,000 for 1997. To find out how much you can contribute, check the Notice of Assessment that Revenue Canada sent you after your 1997 return was processed. It will tell you how much you can contribute.

If you have under-contributed since 1991, have your tax adviser or financial planner track down how much contribution room you have available. If you want to do it yourself, just check out the Revenue Canada listing in the Blue Pages (Grey Pages in Manitoba) of your phone book. Look for the TIPS phone number. You should have last year's tax return and your social security number handy, plus a pen and paper. This amount should also appear on your most recent Notice of Assessment from Revenue Canada.

RPP, DPSP members

If you are a member of an RPP or DPSP, your RRSP contribution limit will be reduced by an amount called the pension adjustment (PA). This adjustment represents the present value of the pension benefits you earned for the previous year in your RPP or DPSP. PA reporting is required as part of the T4 reporting process in February of each year.

Another thing to consider is an adjustment made where benefits are enhanced for post-1989 service. This particular adjustment — the past service pension adjustment (PSPA) — reduces your RRSP contribution limit for any given year. In general, your maximum deduction for any one year will be calculated as follows: RRSP contribution room carried forward **(see article 45)**, plus 18% of your prior year's earned income (to a stated maximum), less your PA for the prior year, less any PSPA for the current year.

EXAMPLE
Adjustments and your RRSP

If your earned income for 1997 was $40,000, and a PA of $2,200 was reported on your 1997 T4, you will be able to contribute $5,000 to an RRSP in 1998 — 18% of $40,000 = $7,200 less the $2,200 PA. However, if a $3,000 PSPA was also reported on your 1998 T4, you would only be able to contribute $2,000 to your RRSP in 1998 — 18% of $40,000 = $7,200 less the $2,200 PA and less the $3,000 PSPA.

Pension adjustment reversals

For members of a RPP or DPSP who leave before retirement, the pension entitlement received is often less than the RRSP contribution room that was given up in favour of the pension plan. The 1997 federal budget recognized this inequity and introduced a pension adjustment reversal (PAR), which is intended to restore lost RRSP contribution room to individuals who leave an RPP or DPSP before retirement.

Generally, the PAR increases the RRSP contribution limit by the amount by which the PAs exceed the termination benefit — thereby restoring the RRSP room that would otherwise be lost. The PAR applies for terminations in 1997 and subsequent years, and RPP or DPSP administrators will have to report the PAR to Revenue Canada.

PARs for terminations in 1997 and 1998 may have to be reported as early as the end of 1998. The PAR will be added to the RRSP deduction room for the year of termination, except for terminations in 1997, which will be added in 1998.

EXAMPLE

Applying the PAR

Suppose you were laid off by your employer in 1997, and based on your earned income for that year your 1998 RRSP contribution room was $13,500. If your former employer reports a PAR of $5,000 in respect to your participation in its pension plan, your 1998 RRSP deduction room will be increased to $18,500.

Age limits

Subject to age restrictions, you may contribute any amount up to your maximum to your RRSP, an RRSP set up for your spouse, or a combination of both. A contribution cannot be made to an RRSP if the beneficiary of the RRSP is 70 years of age or older at the end of 1998. However, if you have earned income and your spouse will be under 70 years of age at the end of the year, you can still make a contribution to your spouse's plan even if you are 70 years of age or older.

Converting your RRSP

Normally, you have until March 1, 1999, to make your 1998 contribution. However, if the beneficiary of the plan turned 69 in 1998, the contribution must be made by December 31, 1998. That's because RRSPs must be converted into a Registered Retirement Income Fund (RRIF) or life or term annuity by December 31 of the year in which the beneficiary turns 69.

A huge word of warning — if you turned 69 in 1998, and your RRSP is not converted into one of these plans by December 31, 1998, the full amount of the RRSP will be brought into your income, and you could incur a substantial tax bill on the additional income. Not only that, your entitlement to Old Age Security benefits may be drastically reduced.

For a taxpayer who dies in 1998, the executor or legal representative can, until March 1, 1999, make a spousal RRSP contribution on behalf of the deceased.

▶ TAX TIPS

If you turned 69 in 1998, you may be able to make an extra contribution for 1999 to your RRSP before collapsing the plan at the end of 1998. Just before you wind it up in 1998, make a contribution equal to your 1999 contribution room. The amount of your 1999 contribution room is based on your 1998 earned income. Payments can then be claimed as a deduction in 1999. This tax-planning tip requires that you have contribution room available for 1999 (i.e., based on your 1998 earned income), and you should discuss it with your tax adviser before proceeding. It is important to note that the contribution may trigger a 1% per month penalty from the date of the contribution to December 31, 1998 **(see article 44)**. Therefore, it would be wise to make this extra contribution in December 1998.

Before proceeding with this option, you and your tax adviser should review your financial situation carefully in light of contribution room, the amount of contribution, penalty tax, etc. You still have the opportunity in the future to contribute to a spousal RRSP if you have earned income and your spouse is under 70 years of age.

43. RRSP CONTRIBUTION LIMITS

The RRSP contribution limit is currently $13,500 and will remain at this level until 2003. After that time, it will be increased to $14,500 in 2004 and $15,500 in 2005. For money purchase RPPs, the maximum limits are also frozen at $13,500 until 2002. After that the limit will rise to $14,500 in 2003 and $15,500 in 2004. Contributions to defined benefit RPPs are not restricted by dollar amounts but the entitlement under such plans is limited to defined levels that approximate the limits for money purchase RPPs.

After 2004 (2005 for RRSPs), the maximum limits are to be adjusted for the annual increase in the average industrial wage.

▶ TAX TIP

To make the most effective use of your RRSP, there are several things you could and should do. It's a good idea to contribute to your RRSP early in the year rather than at the end of the contribution year – that way you can take advantage of income sheltering and compounding a full year earlier. If you make regular contributions to an RRSP, consider applying to have your income tax withholdings reduced on your paycheque – this will improve your monthly cash flow. Even though your RRSP administration fee is no longer tax-deductible, you should consider paying it directly, instead of from inside your RRSP – this helps maintain capital in your plan, allowing it to grow unfettered. You do not need to deduct your contribution in the year it is made. If you are expecting to be in a higher tax bracket in the future, consider delaying your deduction until that time – you will receive a larger tax savings if the deduction is taken when you are in a higher tax bracket. And last, but not least, consider filing tax returns for children or other low income earners to create contribution room that may be used in the future.

44. RRSP OVERCONTRIBUTIONS

Starting with the 1991 tax year, individuals 18 years of age or over were allowed to overcontribute a cumulative lifetime total of $8,000 to their RRSP. This was possible without incurring a penalty tax. The 1995 federal budget significantly altered the rules in this area. As of January 1, 1996, this allowable limit was reduced to $2,000, with an additional allowance provided to an individual who had an overcontribution on February 26, 1995.

An overcontribution is not deductible from income in the current year, but the advantage lies in that you can inject extra cash into your RRSP where it can compound on a pre-tax basis for as long as it remains in the plan. Overcontributions may be deducted in a subsequent year when an actual RRSP contribution is less than the maximum allowed. As of January 1, 1996, the penalty tax of 1% per month applies to the amount of any overcontribution in excess of $2,000 subject to the exception for the additional allowance.

Know your limit

An additional allowance is provided for individuals who had an overcontribution on February 26, 1995. If an overcontribution in excess of $2,000 existed on that date, the monthly penalty tax will not be imposed commencing January 1996. This is provided that the overcontribution did not exceed $8,000 and it is used against available RRSP contribution room for 1996 and subsequent years until the overcontribution is reduced to $2,000.

▶ *TAX TIPS*

Before overcontributing to an RRSP, you are usually better off to pay down debt on which interest is not deductible, such as a large outstanding personal credit card balance or a personal home mortgage. Check with your tax or financial adviser to determine your best course of action. If you decide to overcontribute, work with your adviser to ensure you stay within the allowable limit. One of the reasons the government permits an overcontribution is to provide you with a cushion against possible errors and unforeseen events.

Consider using your $2,000 overcontribution when you quit working. The earned income you have in your final year of employment will entitle you to an RRSP deduction in the following year.

45. RRSP CARRY-FORWARD RULES

Revenue Canada recognizes that for many individuals, it is not always possible to make a full RRSP contribution in any given year. To remedy this situation, it allows you to carry forward the unused portion of your contribution room to subsequent years. That means if you were eligible to contribute $10,000 to an RRSP each year from 1991 to 1997 but only contributed $7,000 each year, you will be able to contribute an additional $21,000 over and above your annual maximum contribution limit.

If you expect a change in your income in the near future — a change that might see you bumped up into a higher tax bracket — it might make sense to consider delaying your RRSP contributions until that time. However, you must also consider the loss of tax-sheltered investment growth by building up your RRSP later rather than earlier.

▶ *TAX TIPS*

In order to accumulate RRSP contribution room, you must file an income tax return. If you have "earned income" for RRSP purposes but you are not required to file an income tax return, you should consider filing a return anyway. While an RRSP may not be a significant consideration at this point, there will probably be a time when you have sufficient cash to make a contribution and benefit from the deduction.

Will you have low taxable income in 1998, unused contribution room and enough excess cash to make an RRSP contribution? Then consider making the contribution for 1998 but not claiming the deduction on your 1998 return. As long as the amount is not claimed as a deduction, your unused contribution room will remain intact. You can still claim the deduction in a future year, preferably when your taxable income is higher. In the meantime, the investments in the RRSP will compound tax-free.

46. SELF-DIRECTED RRSPs

Self-directed RRSPs are subject to special rules. Despite the annual administration fee — which unfortunately is no longer tax-deductible — a self-directed RRSP will give you more flexibility and may provide you with the opportunity to realize better returns. However, you should have a little time to give it the attention it needs.

In a self-directed plan, you make your own investment choices. These decisions can be based on information given to you by your tax or financial adviser. In fact, many Canadians allow their financial planners to look after their self-directed plans. However, as the owner of the plan, you always have the final say in how it's managed and the types of investments purchased.

Should your plan acquire a non-qualified investment, the value of that investment is included as income on your return. Additional taxes may apply on foreign property acquired by the plan. You are also restricted in the amount of foreign investments you can hold in your RRSP — currently it is limited to 20%.

Transferring investments

You may transfer other investments you own into your self-directed RRSP as part of your deductible contribution. Or you may sell them to your plan. Should their fair market value at the time of the transfer or sale exceed your cost, the difference must be reported as a capital gain. However, you are out of luck if your cost exceeds the fair market value — you cannot deduct the capital loss. It then stands to reason that it is not the best idea to sell or transfer losing investments to your RRSP. It is also possible to hold the mortgage on your home in your RRSP — it takes a little bit to set up, and there are costs involved, but this arrangement can offer some advantages.

EXAMPLE

Investment transfers

In your quest for financial independence, you acquired 100 shares of ABC Co. in 1996 for $10 per share. Now, a few years later in February 1999, you are considering a contribution to your RRSP and are reviewing your available options. If the shares of ABC are trading at $15 per share and you transfer all of the shares to your RRSP, your RRSP contribution will be $1,500 and you will report a capital gain of $500 — in other words, $1,500 less the original $1,000 cost of the investment.

Now if those shares are trading at $8 per share, your RRSP contribution will be $800 but you will not be able to claim a capital loss of $200 ($800 - $1,000) on the transfer. As an alternative, you could sell your shares for $8 per share and contribute the cash proceeds to your RRSP. That being the case, your RRSP contribution will still be $800, but you may be able to claim the $200 capital loss.

▶ TAX TIP

If you have a self-directed RRSP, transferring your investments to it may be a way to get your annual RRSP contribution writeoff without actually laying out any cash. However, there are some drawbacks to holding shares in an RRSP. Since shares pay dividend income, which is tax-preferred, it might make more sense to keep these investments outside of your RRSP and fill up your contribution room with investments that generate interest – savings bonds, GICs, etc. – which are usually taxed at a less advantaged rate.

In recent years, the types of investments that can be held by your self-directed RRSP have been expanded. In certain situations your RRSP can invest in a Canadian private company if it carries on its business primarily in Canada. Certain types of business activities do not qualify. However, the rules are extremely complicated and you should be aware of how they may affect your potential investment before your RRSP acquires it. Talk to a knowledgeable adviser first.

When considering long-term investments such as five-year guaranteed investment certificates (GICs) within your RRSP, keep in mind that you may have a sticky problem if you need to withdraw the funds before the investment matures.

47. RETIRING ALLOWANCES AND RRSPs

Individuals who will receive or have received an amount from their former employers upon dismissal or retirement in 1998 may be eligible to contribute an extra amount to their RRSP or RPP. These retiring allowances are a key item in personal tax planning. They are attractive because they are also deductible for the payer. In addition, amounts transferred to your RRSP or RPP are not taxable until they are withdrawn from the plan.

What amounts are involved?

The maximum amount that can be transferred to your RRSP or RPP is $2,000 times the number of years you worked for your employer before 1996. Also add in $1,500 times the number of years you were employed prior to 1989 in which your employer did not make vested contributions to a registered plan on your behalf. Note that the contribution, which is in addition to your regular contribution limit, must be made to your own retirement plan, and not your spouse's.

Under new rules proposed for 1998 and subsequent years, RRSP rollovers and contributions, as well as contributions to RPPs, will not be a factor in calculating the alternative minimum tax (AMT). If you were subject to the AMT in one or more of the years from 1994 to 1997 (as a result of an RRSP or RPP deduction), the amount of AMT attributed to the RRSP deduction will be refunded to you. Of course this will be to the extent you had not already recovered the AMT **(see article 110)**.

> ▶*TAX TIP*
> If the portion of your retiring allowance that is eligible to be transferred to your RRSP is paid directly to your RRSP, it is imperative that you complete form TD2 — a tax deduction waiver in respect of funds to be transferred. This way, your employer will not be obligated to withhold income tax.

48. RRSPs AND LOANS

Before November 13, 1981, interest on loans taken out to invest in an RRSP was, and continues to be, deductible. However, interest on similar loans taken out on and after that date is not deductible. Therefore, your investments should be structured to take maximum advantage of the interest deductibility rules.

▶ *TAX TIP*
Consider cashing in an existing investment to contribute to your RRSP and then, if you wish, borrowing funds to acquire another investment. This way you receive a deduction for your RRSP contribution, and the interest on the loan borrowed for investment purposes is also tax deductible.

49. TRANSFER OF PENSION INCOME

Are you entitled to a lump-sum payment out of a registered pension plan (RPP) or a deferred profit sharing plan (DPSP)? Then that amount may be contributed to another RPP, DPSP or RRSP. However, the lump-sum payment must be made directly from one plan to another, and then only if certain conditions are met.

Certain lump-sum payments or withdrawals from foreign plans — such as U.S. individual retirement accounts (IRA) — can also be contributed to your RRSP tax-free. However, a similar deferral of foreign tax may not be available on the transfer. Have your adviser explore all the options and potential tax obligations of such transfers.

50. USING AN RRSP TO BUY A HOME

The Home Buyer's Plan, introduced in February 1992, allows you to withdraw up to $20,000 from your RRSP as a loan without paying tax. Originally a one-year measure, it was extended one year until it expired on March 1, 1994. However, a modified and less complicated form of the plan has been introduced in its place.

Under the new plan, again it is first-time home buyers who will be eligible for participation. You are considered to be a first-time buyer if neither you nor your spouse has owned a house and lived in it for the five years preceding the withdrawal. Loan repayments must take place over a period of 15 years, or less if desired. If the required repayment is not made, an amount will have to be included as income in the year of the repayment shortfall.

▶ *TAX TIP*
If you contribute an amount to your RRSP, you cannot make a withdrawal under the Home Buyer's Plan within 90 days of that contribution, or your ability to claim a deduction for the contribution may be restricted. As a general rule, you should make your RRSP contribution more than 90 days before the withdrawal. After a wait of 90 days or more, your deduction may

generate a refund, which can then also be applied towards your down payment.

In a related move, if you have money on hand for a down payment, and you have accumulated some RRSP contribution room, open up an RRSP. Then you can deposit the money into the plan, wait 90 days, be eligible to partake in the Home Buyer's program, and at the same time use whatever refund is issued to bolster your original down payment amount. Be sure to run this by your tax adviser to ensure that it is a sound strategy for your particular financial circumstances.

For an individual who previously participated in the Home Buyer's Plan, the 1998 federal budget proposes that, in specified circumstances, he or she will able to participate a second time. The provision is that the full amount previously withdrawn must be paid back into the RRSP before the beginning of the given year in which the individual wishes to participate a second time. The participant must still qualify as a first-time home buyer. This proposal applies for 1999 and subsequent years.

Persons with disabilities

An existing home owner who has a disability or is a relative of a person who has a disability may withdraw funds from his or her RRSP under the Home Buyer's Plan, if the withdrawal is to assist the individual or the disabled relative to purchase a home.

Some conditions must be met first:

- the individual or the disabled relative must qualify for the "disability credit" **(see article 67)**
- the home must be more accessible for, or better suited for, the care of the disabled individual
- if the owner is not disabled, the disabled relative must live in the home

This proposal also applies to withdrawals in 1999 and subsequent years.

▶ *TAX TIP*

Each spouse can withdraw eligible amounts under the Home Buyer's Plan from any of their respective RRSPs, including spousal RRSPs. Also, each spouse can withdraw up to the $20,000 limit or $40,000 in aggregate (if purchasing the property jointly).

51. USING AN RRSP TO FINANCE HIGHER EDUCATION

The 1998 federal budget proposes to allow RRSP withdrawals be made to finance the pursuit of higher education. Eligible individuals will be able to make tax-free withdrawals from their RRSPs to finance full-time training or education for themselves or their spouses. Withdrawals will be limited to $10,000 per year, over a period of up to four calendar years, and subject to a combined total of $20,000.

In order to qualify, the individual or the individual's spouse must be enrolled in a qualifying education program — which must be at least three months in duration — at an eligible educational institution. Disabled students may qualify whether or not they are studying full time.

Withdrawals must be repaid to the RRSP over a maximum 10-year period starting in the year after the last year that the individual was enrolled as a full-time student. However, the repayments must commence no later than the sixth year after the initial withdrawal, even if the individual continues to be enrolled on a full-time basis. If the required repayment is not made, an amount will have to be included in income. As with many tax situations, special rules apply.

52. DEATH AND THE RRSP

Should you die while you still own your RRSP, its entire value must be included in your income in the year of your death unless your spouse or, if you have no spouse, your financially dependent children or grandchildren, are entitled to the funds.

As part of the terms of your RRSP, you may designate your spouse as beneficiary of the plan in the event of your death. The proceeds from the plan will be taxable in your spouse's hands in the year they are received, unless transferred into his or her own RRSP. Funds can also be transferred into a registered retirement income fund (RRIF) or be used to purchase an eligible annuity. In all three cases, no taxes will be payable until funds are withdrawn from the RRSP, RRIF or annuity.

If your spouse is not the designated beneficiary of your RRSP, its value may still be taxable in your spouse's hands upon your death, provided he or she is a beneficiary of your estate. This approach may provide more flexibility, but more paperwork will be involved.

For the purpose of these rules, "spouse" is an individual of the opposite sex who cohabited with the deceased taxpayer and who either cohabited for at least one year or is the parent of the deceased's child. Other rules apply if you die after your plan has matured and you were receiving annuity payments from your RRSP or RRIF.

53. RETIREMENT AND THE RRSP

Considering withdrawing funds from your RRSP? Then you should be aware of options available to you.

You are required to take the funds out of your RRSP by the end of the calendar year in which you reach the age of 69. When you collapse your RRSP, you may transfer the funds free of tax into a Registered Retirement Income Fund (RRIF) or a life or term annuity. The third option is to withdraw the funds and pay tax on the full amount. The choice will be based upon your retirement objectives, tax implications and your cash flow requirements.

How RRIFs work

A RRIF provides you with varying amounts of income during retirement. If the payments are structured properly, a RRIF can continue indefinitely, essentially providing income for life. Payments from a RRIF are quite flexible. You can withdraw as much as you want, although you must take a minimum amount each year. The minimum amount increases slightly, based on a specific formula, each year as you age. It increases incrementally from about 4.76% at age 69 to 20% at age 94 and older. RRIF payments are subject to tax in the year of receipt.

How annuities work

If your RRSP funds are transferred to an annuity, periodic payments from the annuity will also be taxed in the year of receipt. Annuities can be arranged to provide payments for either a fixed term (for example, to age 90) or for life. The main advantage to an annuity is that you can have some form of guarantee with respect to the amounts you will receive.

For instance, if you opt for a life annuity, you and/or your spouse can be guaranteed a specific income stream regardless of how long either of you survives. Nevertheless, an annuity is not as flexible as a RRIF. Once you purchase a life annuity and the funds are deposited and registered, they are locked in. You generally cannot de-register or cash in the plan at any time, or amend the terms of the contract.

Tax implications

If you withdraw funds from your RRSP you will pay tax on the amount withdrawn. This will result in immediate taxation at your marginal tax rate. There are many options available to you when you decide to cash in your RRSP. Become familiar with the various alternatives and their tax consequences; that way you'll be able to make an informed and pertinent choice.

▶ **TAX TIP**

Depending on your income, you should consider the pros and cons of withdrawing funds from your RRSP before you reach the age of 65. The additional income will be subject to income tax at your marginal tax rate. However, if you receive income from your RRSP after you are 65, in addition to being taxed at your marginal tax rate it may also reduce your eligibility at that time for the OAS benefit.

54. OLD AGE SECURITY CLAWBACK

The government imposes a special tax — the "clawback" — on your Old Age Security (OAS) payments if your net income for the year is in excess of a certain annual threshold amount. Currently that stands at $53,215. The amount of the clawback is equal to the lesser of your OAS payments and 15% of the amount by which your net income exceeds the threshold amount. From July 1996, the clawback amounts have been recovered through withholdings from monthly OAS payments.

How it works

The reduction in the monthly payments for the period from January through June is based on your net income from two years ago. The reduction in the payments for July to December is based on your net income from last year.

Suppose your net income was $56,000 in 1996 and $58,000 in 1997. Your 1996 net income exceeds the threshold by $2,785, resulting in a projected OAS overpayment of $418 (15% x $2,785). Your payments for January 1998 through June 1998 are each reduced by $35 ($418/12).

Your 1997 net income exceeds the threshold by $4,785, resulting in a projected OAS overpayment of $718 (15% x $4,785). Your payments for July 1998 through December 1998 will each be reduced by $60 ($718/12).

When you file your 1998 income tax return, Revenue Canada will calculate the actual OAS clawback based on your net income for the year. This amount will be compared to amounts withheld from monthly payments during the year. Any excess withheld will be refunded or applied against any other tax liability. Conversely, where the amount withheld falls short, you will be required to remit the difference.

> ▶ *TAX TIPS*
>
> If you are just over the $53,215 clawback threshold and your spouse's net income is below it, consider splitting your Canada Pension Plan (CPP) benefits with your spouse if that will bring your net income below the limit **(see article 76)**.
>
> If you are considering making the election to include all of your spouse's taxable Canadian dividends in your income **(see article 99)**, ensure that you are not subjecting yourself to the OAS clawback by using this strategy.

55. CHILDCARE EXPENSES

Because of work commitments, you or your spouse (or other supporting individual) may qualify to deduct eligible expenses for day care and/or other forms of childcare. Eligible costs include day care or babysitting, boarding school and camp expenses. Medical expenses, tuition, clothing or transportation expenses are not eligible. You are also not allowed to deduct payments made to persons who are under 18 years of age and related to you. As with most qualifying expenses accepted by Revenue Canada, there is a specified limit.

Who can claim?

In typical circumstances, where the child lives with both parents, the parent with the lower net income must claim the expense deduction. A parent with no income is considered to have the lower income and, therefore, will be the parent who is required to claim the expenses. The supporting parent with the higher income may only claim a deduction for that period during which the lower-income spouse is infirm, confined to a bed or a wheelchair, attending a secondary school or a designated educational institution, or incarcerated in a correctional facility.

Prior to 1996, the lower-income spouse was required to be in full-time attendance at a designated educational institution. This requirement has now been relaxed. However, there are minimum program duration requirements that must be met. Special rules also apply for parents who have separated during the year or are divorced.

How much can you deduct?

You can generally deduct up to $5,000 annually for each child who is six years of age or under at the end of the year and for each child who is dependent by reason of mental or physical infirmity. You can also deduct up to $3,000 for each child aged seven to fifteen at any time in the year. The total deduction cannot exceed two-thirds of the salary or business income of the parent who is required to claim the deduction.

Changes are on hand

The 1998 federal budget has proposed that, effective in 1998 and subsequent years, the $5,000 limit be increased to $7,000 and the $3,000 limit increased to $4,000.

EXAMPLE

Deducting childcare expenses

You and your spouse are both employed and earn $15,000 and $65,000 per year, respectively. Also assume you incurred $10,000 in eligible childcare expenses in 1998 for your only child, a five-year-old. Since your income is less than your spouse's, you are the spouse entitled to deduct the childcare expenses. The maximum you can deduct is the lesser of $7,000 and two-thirds of your net income (2/3 x $15,000 = $10,000). Therefore, you can deduct $7,000 of childcare expenses in 1998.

Special rules introduced in 1996 allow single parents to deduct childcare expenses against all types of income if the parent attends school full-time. A similar rule will apply to two-parent families when both parents are attending school full-time at the same time.

Along with the main changes proposed by the 1998 budget is the ability for single parents to claim a deduction in respect to childcare expenses for those months in which they study part-time. It applies for 1998 and subsequent years, and this expense will be deductible against all types of income. In a two-parent family, where one parent studies part-time, the higher income earner will be allowed to claim the childcare expenses, within certain limits, while the other spouse is studying.

56. ALIMONY AND MAINTENANCE

Rules regarding alimony and maintenance payments changed significantly as of May 1, 1997. The new system provides separate tax treatment for child support payments and spousal support payments. In effect, the changes apply to child support payments while the tax treatment of spousal support payments remains unchanged. Periodic payments for spousal support continue to be taxable to the recipient and deductible by the payer.

What's changed?

For new or varied child support agreements made after April 30, 1997, the recipient will not pay tax on the payments and the payer will not receive a tax deduction for them. If the agreement or order does not identify an amount as being solely for the support of a spouse, it will be treated as child support. Similarly, any third-party payments that are not clearly identified as being solely for the benefit of the spouse will be treated as child support.

The new rules also apply, in some situations, to older agreements and orders. A case in point is where a previous order or agreement is varied or amended after April 30, 1997, and results in a change in the amount of child support. The new rules also apply where an order or agreement entered into before May 1, 1997, specifies that the new rules are to apply from a given date. In addition, parties to an agreement or order entered into before May 1, 1997, may jointly elect to have the new rules apply.

▶ *TAX TIP*
If you are party to an agreement or order entered into before May 1, 1997, and you want the new rules to apply, you must jointly elect by filing form

T1157. In some cases you may also be required to file a copy of the agreement itself.

Registration of Agreements

In some cases, you or your spouse may be required to file form T1158, along with a copy of the agreement or court order, with Revenue Canada. Generally, these requirements extend to situations in which payments will continue to be deductible — for example, if an agreement is entered into after May 1, 1997, and it contains a requirement for either spousal payments only, or for separate amounts for spousal and child support. Agreements entered into before May 1, 1997, may also have to be filed if they provide for spousal or spousal and child support payments and the agreement becomes subject to the new rules. Your tax adviser will be able to provide details to you on these filing requirements.

Child support payments from a resident of the United States are not taxable under the Canada-U.S. tax treaty.

Alimony/maintenance stay the same

Generally, the rules remain unchanged for alimony and maintenance payments made pursuant to a written separation agreement or court order in place before May 1, 1997. These amounts are deductible for tax purposes if they meet certain criteria. Also, if the spouse making the payments is allowed to deduct them, the spouse receiving the payments must include the amounts in income.

To be deductible, payments must be periodic, for the maintenance of your spouse and/or children, and made pursuant to a written separation agreement or court order. Payments made in the same year (as well as those in the preceding year) before the agreement was signed may also be deductible, provided the agreement or court order recognizes these payments.

Support payments arising from the breakdown of a common-law relationship may also be deductible. The requirements for deductibility by the payer and taxability to the recipient are similar to those discussed for separation or divorce, except that a court order (rather than a separation agreement) is required. If the court order was made before February 11, 1988, the payer can deduct the amounts and the recipient will pay tax on them provided both parties have elected to have this rule apply.

Third-party rules

Rules have also been established regarding the tax treatment of alimony and maintenance payments that have been paid to a third party rather than directly to the spouse or former spouse. Such payments, which can include medical bills, tuition fees and mortgage payments, may qualify for a deduction and corresponding income inclusion. To qualify, the expense must have been incurred at a time when the payer and the recipient were separated and living apart, and such payments must have been specifically provided for in the court order or written agreement.

57. MOVING EXPENSES

If you moved from one location in Canada to another in 1998, you may qualify to deduct your eligible moving expenses on your 1998 return. You must have started work or carried on a business at your new location. In addition, your new residence must be at least 40 kilometres closer to your new work location. A recent court case concluded that this distance should be measured using the shortest normal route open to the travelling public.

Costs you can claim

Eligible moving expenses include travelling expenses incurred in connection with the move and the cost of transporting your household goods. Also, the cost of meals and temporary accommodation for a period not exceeding 15 days is eligible, as are the costs of selling your old residence, or if you were renting, the cost of breaking your lease. Any loss incurred on the sale of your former residence cannot be deducted.

With the 1998 budget, the federal government has proposed to expand the list of eligible moving expenses. They include mortgage interest, property taxes, insurance premiums and costs associated with maintaining heat and power — to a maximum of $5,000 — payable in respect of a vacant former residence. This will be in effect for a period that begins after 1997, does not exceed three months, and during which all reasonable efforts are made to sell the former residence. The cost of revising legal documents to reflect the taxpayer's new address, replacing driving licences and automobile permits, and having utilities connected and/or disconnected, are also now eligible for deduction. Again, these measures apply to expenses incurred after 1997.

Moving expenses paid for by your employer cannot be claimed by you as a deduction. If your employer pays or reimburses you for part of your moving expenses, you may deduct all of your eligible moving expenses but must report the amounts paid by your employer as income. Eligible expenses are only deductible from the income earned at the new location. Amounts not deducted in the year of the move may be carried forward to the next year.

▶*TAX TIP*

If you are moving to a new work location, any relocation payments should be clearly structured as a reimbursement. Payments received as a blanket lump sum allowance, rather than a reimbursement of costs already incurred, may leave you open to tax implications. A chat with your tax adviser should determine how the payments can be structured to avoid or minimize tax.

Reimbursement vs. allowance

Numerous court cases have addressed the tax status of amounts received following relocation for employment. As these cases reach the higher courts, the distinction between a "reimbursement" and an "allowance" is often the critical factor. It is Revenue Canada's position that employees who are compensated by their employers for the higher costs associated with moving to a new work location (for example, higher house prices) must include the amount received in income.

However, if your employer reimburses you for a loss incurred on the sale of your former residence, the amount was not normally required to be included in income. Under certain conditions, employers could reimburse the mortgage interest differential on an employee's new home, and that amount did not have to be included in income. That now is about to change.

The 1998 federal budget proposes that all subsidies paid directly or indirectly by an employer in respect of the financing of an employee's new or former residence will be taxable. Also one-half of amounts in excess of $15,000 paid directly or indirectly to an employee by an employer to compensate for a loss on disposition of the former residence will be taxable. These two changes will be effective in 2001 for employees who begin working in the new location before October 1998 (i.e., will apply to amounts provided or paid in 2001 and subsequent years). Where employees begin working in the new location after September 1998, the change will apply at the time the benefit is received.

▶ *TAX TIP*

If you have to start a job at a new location, but a permanent move to that area is not possible until the following year, you won't lose any of your eligible deductions because the two events do not coincide. That's because the courts are on your side. They have ruled that where a taxpayer commences employment at a new location but does not move until a subsequent year, the taxpayer has a right to claim moving expenses incurred in that subsequent year.

Student eligibility

Students can also claim moving expenses if they move to begin a job (including summer employment) or to start a business. If the move is to attend a full-time post-secondary institution, you can deduct the expenses, but only to the extent of your scholarship or research grant income.

EXAMPLE
Students' deductions

A budding academic, you live in Charlottetown and the University of British Columbia has offered you a $750 scholarship for the 1998 school year. You subsequently decide to attend full-time courses at that university and purchase an airline ticket for $1,000. Since you must include in income all scholarships and similar awards received in the year to the extent that the total of such amounts exceeds $500, you must include $250 in income in 1998. As a result, you will be able to deduct up to $250 of the cost of the airline ticket in 1998. If the amount is not claimed in 1998, you may be able to deduct it from scholarship or research grant income in 1999.

58. WHAT IS A TAX CREDIT?

Several of the articles that follow refer to a tax credit. And although there is a substantial difference between a tax credit and a tax deduction, it is easy to get the two confused. Items that are deductible reduce your taxable income, with the actual amount of tax saved depending on your personal tax rate. If you are in the highest tax bracket, the deduction is generally worth a little more than 50 cents on the dollar. If you are in the lowest bracket, it is worth about 27 cents on the dollar. If you have no taxable income, a deduction may not save you any tax at all.

A tax credit, on the other hand is a deduction from tax owing. Provided the credit can be used, each taxpayer receives the same tax relief from a tax credit, regardless of his or her particular tax bracket.

In all provinces except Quebec, personal income tax is calculated as a percentage of federal tax. Most tax credits that reduce federal tax also reduce the applicable provincial tax. To calculate the real value of the tax credit, you should add the provincial saving. A rough rule of thumb is to add 50% to the amount of the federal credit to calculate the real tax reduction.

EXAMPLE

What they are worth

Assume you live in a province where the provincial tax rate is 50% and you are in the highest tax bracket (29%). Your combined federal and provincial marginal tax rate in 1998 will be 43.5% [29% + (50% x 29%)], ignoring surtaxes. A $100 tax deduction will save you $43.50 in tax. Your tax savings will be dependent on the tax bracket you are in. However, most tax credits are calculated using the lowest federal rate of tax (17%). Therefore, if you have an amount of $100 that is eligible for a tax credit, you will save $25.50 in tax [17% + (50% x 17%) x $100].

59. TAX CREDITS FOR CHARITABLE DONATIONS

Donations made to registered charities, registered Canadian amateur athletic associations, Canadian municipalities, the federal government or a provincial government are eligible for a tax credit that reduces the taxes you have to pay. As a general rule, donations to U.S. charitable organizations qualify for the credit provided you also have U.S. source net income that is taxable in Canada.

Without exception, donations may be claimed only after they are paid — pledges do not count. Prior to 1996, most claims for gifts to charities were limited to 20% of your net income for the year. Unused claims may be carried forward for up to five years and donations made in the year of death may be carried back one year.

Limits to rise again

With the 1996 budget, the federal government increased the general annual limit on charitable donations as a percentage of net income to 50% (100% in the year of death or the preceding year). These limits were further increased in the 1997 budget to 75% of net income. The limit on gifts by individuals in the year of death (and prior year) remains at the 1996 limit of 100%. Starting in 1997, donations to the federal or provincial governments were subject to the same general limit of 75% of net income. Such donations were previously 100% creditable.

Save those receipts

To secure the credit, you must include the original official receipts issued by the registered charity or association with your tax return. These receipts will include the registration number of the given institution. Photocopies of receipts are not acceptable, and filing cancelled cheques is not sufficient either. If you are filing your return electronically **(see article 129)** or by using TELEFILE **(see article 130)** you are not required to file these receipts with your return, but you must retain them for future audit purposes.

The credit is 17% on the first $200 of donations claimed in the year, and 29% on the amount in excess of $200. After factoring in provincial tax savings, donations in excess of $200 will save you approximately 44% to 54% (depending on your province of residence).

▶ TAX TIP

If you and your spouse donate over $200 in any one year, the tax credit will be larger if one spouse claims the entire amount. That way, there is only the one $200 amount to be credited at 17%, instead of two claims. Donation receipts normally are accepted if claimed on either spouse's return.

EXAMPLE
Joining forces
Suppose you donated $400 in 1998 and your spouse donated $600. Rather than claim individually, where each of you receives a 17% credit on the first $200, you should pool the amounts and have one of you claim it. That way you receive a 17% credit on $200, and a 29% credit on $800. Doing it separately would mean you will only get a 29% credit on $600.

Donating property
If you donate capital property to a registered charity, you can elect to value the gift at any amount up to its fair market value. The amount that is claimed as a donation must also be reported as your proceeds of disposition of the property.

For 1997 and subsequent years, the general annual limit of 75% of net income is increased by 25% of the taxable capital gain included in income from the donated property. This effectively allows 100% of the donor's taxable income created by the disposition to be offset by tax credits.

In the 1997 federal budget two other changes relating to the donation of capital property were proposed. First, the income inclusion rate on capital gains arising from the donation of eligible property to a charity (other than a private charitable foundation) made after February 18, 1997, and before 2002, will be reduced to 37.5% from 75%. Eligible property includes securities, such as shares and bonds — listed on a prescribed stock exchange — as well as mutual fund units.

Second, donors of depreciable assets, such as buildings and equipment, will be entitled to increase the net income limit for such a donation by 25% of the recaptured depreciation arising from the donation. This increase, combined with the increase in the general limit of 25% of the taxable capital gain arising from the donation, will ensure that the donor has enough tax credits to more than offset the tax arising from both the recaptured depreciation and taxable capital gain. This takes effect for donations made after 1996.

EXAMPLE

Sharing the wealth

Your net income in 1998 was $125,000, and despite talk of mergers (or maybe because of it) you decide to donate all of your bank shares, having a fair market value of $100,000, to a registered charity. When you purchased the shares in 1990, they cost $10,000, and now you have elected to dispose of the shares at their fair market value. This results in a $90,000 capital gain. Your 1998 net income? Here's the outcome:

Net income	$125,000
Taxable capital gain (37.5% x $90,000)	33,750
Total Net Income	$158,750
The donation amount eligible for tax credit is calculated as follows:	
75% of net income	$119,063
25% of taxable capital gain	8,437
Limit	$127,500
Available for credit (donation amount)	$100,000
Assuming your marginal tax rate is 50%, the tax saving arising from the donation is:	
Tax on the taxable capital gain (50% x $33,750)	$ 16,875
Tax savings from donation credit (50% x $100,000)	50,000
Overall tax savings	$ 33,125

The $16,875 tax liability, arising from the donation of the property, is more than offset by the $50,000 tax savings arising from the donation.

▶*TAX TIP*

With the increases in donation limits, it may not be necessary to elect proceeds at an amount lower than the fair market value of the property to eliminate a current tax liability arising from the donation.

Taxpayers, including artists, who donate their works of art to a charity, public art gallery or other public institution, may qualify for special tax treatment.

Other gifts

Donations do not always have to be in the form of money or tangible property. The donation of a life insurance policy to a registered charitable organization qualifies for the credit, provided certain conditions are met. The amount eligible for the credit is the cash surrender value of the policy and any accumulated dividends and interest at the time of the transfer. Under certain conditions, the gift of a residual interest in a trust or estate may also qualify for the credit. Your tax adviser can provide additional information in these areas.

60. POLITICAL DONATIONS

Contributions made to registered political parties generate tax credits (within limits), not tax deductions. Political contributions to federal parties can only be applied against federal income taxes. The credit is calculated as follows: 75% of the first $100, 50% on the next $450 and 33 1/3% of any contribution over $550. The maximum credit allowed in any one year is $500, which means that you do not receive credit for political contributions over $1,150. Some provinces provide similar credits against provincial income taxes for contributions made to provincial political parties. To claim the credit you must attach a copy of the receipt to your return.

For both federal and provincial purposes, the credit may reduce only taxes paid or payable. If you are not liable for any taxes in 1998, the credit is lost. It cannot be carried forward to 1999.

▶ *TAX TIP*
Consider spreading your political contributions over two years. For example, if you contribute $700 in 1998, your federal tax credit will be $350. If instead you contribute $350 in 1998 and $350 in 1999, your political contribution tax credit will be $200 each year for a total of $400.

61. MEDICAL EXPENSES

Medical expenses paid within any 12-month period ending in the year are eligible for a tax credit claim. Expenses reimbursed by either your employer or a private or government-sponsored health care plan are not allowed. The list of eligible expenses is extensive and includes fees paid to a private health or dental plan. You may claim medical expenses for yourself, your spouse and for certain related persons.

▶ *TAX TIP*
The legal representatives of a deceased taxpayer may claim any medical expenses paid – for the year of death – by the taxpayer or his legal repre-

sentative within any 24-month period that includes the date of death. The same expense may not be claimed more than once.

For 1998, total eligible medical expenses must first be reduced by the lesser of two amounts — 3% of your net income, or $1,614. The tax credit is 17% of the amount remaining.

▶ **TAX TIP**
Select your 12-month period to maximize the tax credit. The 12-month period ending in the year may be varied from year to year, but you cannot claim the same expense twice. Keep your receipts for next year if some of your 1998 expenses are not claimed as a credit in 1998.

The 1997 federal budget introduced a refundable medical expense supplement, which is available to eligible individuals who have business or employment income of at least $2,500. The refundable credit is 25% of medical expenses that qualify for the regular medical expense tax credit, up to a maximum of $500. However, it is reduced by 5% of the taxpayer's (and spouse's) income in excess of $16,069. The refundable credit is fully eliminated when combined income exceeds $26,069. This credit is in addition to the tax credit for medical expenses.

62. ATTENDANT FOR A DISABLED PERSON

Disabled persons who incur costs for attendant care that allows the earning of income can deduct these expenses. The deduction is limited to two-thirds of "earned income," which is basically salary and business income.

As an alternative, you can claim the cost of attendant care incurred as a medical expense for purposes of the medical expense tax credit **(see article 61)** even if you are not earning income. The amount eligible for tax credit is $10,000 ($20,000 in the year of death).

▶ **TAX TIP**
If you are disabled and your income is over $29,000, the deduction for attendant care is worth more to you than claiming the medical expense tax credit. You will be further ahead economically by taking the deduction **(see article 58)**.

63. TUITION FEES AND EDUCATION CREDITS

Students are entitled to a tax credit equal to 17% of tuition fees at qualifying educational and training institutions. They are also entitled to an education credit of 17% of $200 per month (or $34.00) for the number of months in the year they were full-time students. This includes full-time post-secondary students enrolled in correspondence courses.

To assist part-time students, the 1998 federal budget proposed an education credit equal to 17% of $60 per month of part-time attendance at a Canadian educational institution. In order to qualify, the student must be enrolled in an eligible program of at least three consecutive weeks duration, with a minimum of 12 course hours each month.

What's covered?

Qualifying fees include those for attending a Canadian university, college or other educational institution providing courses at a post-secondary level. If you attend a primary or secondary school that provides courses at the post-secondary level, you may also qualify for the tuition credit, provided the course paid for is at the post-secondary level. Courses you take to improve or obtain an occupational skill also qualify, provided the institution is certified by the ministry of employment and immigration. In order to qualify for the tuition credit, the total fees for the year paid to each institution must be at least $100. Subject to certain restrictions, tuition fees paid to universities outside Canada also qualify for the credit.

Both the tuition fee credit and the education credit are claimed on a calendar-year basis. All claims for tuition fee credits must be supported by formal receipts. Claims for the $200 per month education credit must be supported by form T2202 or T2202A, which is completed by the educational institution you attend. Currently, you do not have to file these supporting documents with your return, but they must be available if requested by Revenue Canada.

▶ *TAX TIP*
    If you cannot fully utilize your tuition and education tax credits to reduce taxes payable to zero, all or a portion of the unused credits may be transferred to a spouse or supporting parent or grandparent.

Should a student be unable to use all or a portion of a credit, he or she can transfer it to an eligible person up to a $5,000 maximum amount. That translates into an $850 federal tax credit. To make this designation, the student must complete and sign form T2202. A copy of the signed form should be kept by the designated person and if applicable, by the student to support the amount claimed. Currently, the form does not need to be filed with the return but must be available if requested by Revenue Canada.

Prior to 1997, tax credits earned for tuition fees and the education amount were lost if not used by the student or a person to whom they can be transferred. Beginning with credits earned in 1997, students are entitled to carry forward indefinitely unused tuition and education credits. This will enable students to utilize the credit when they have sufficient income. Any amount not used in the current year by the student and not transferred to an eligible person will be automatically available to carry forward. Transfer to an eligible person will continue to be restricted to $5,000 and will be available for credits earned in the current year only.

▶ *TAX TIP*

Students must provide all necessary information to Revenue Canada to establish the carry-forward. This will require filing an income tax return, even if one is not otherwise required.

64. CLAIMING SPOUSE'S UNUSED CREDITS

▶ *TAX TIP*

Does your spouse have little or no taxable income and cannot use all the federal tax credits to which he or she is entitled? Then you are in a position to claim the portion of the qualifying credits that your spouse is unable to use. However, you may not receive a transfer of credits from your spouse if you were separated at the end of the year and if you were separated for a 90-day period that commenced at any time in the year. Unused credits that can be transferred include the tuition fee and education credits **(see article 63)**, the pension credit **(see article 65)**, the disability credit **(see article 67)**, and the age credit **(see article 69)**.

To determine how much your spouse can transfer to you, you must calculate your spouse's federal tax liability before applying any of these credits. Then, you subtract from this amount his or her basic tax credit ($1,098), the supplementary personal tax credit (maximum $42.50 for 1998) **(see article 66 and Table 1)**, and the amount of any tax credits arising from EI or CPP contributions. If there are no federal taxes payable after applying these three credits, then the full amount of his or her unused credits can be transferred to you. If after deducting these credits (basic, supplementary, EI and CPP), your spouse still owes federal tax, the qualifying credits must be applied first to eliminate his or her remaining federal tax liability. The remaining portion can be transferred to you.

EXAMPLE

To your credit

Suppose you earn $100,000 of employment income and your spouse earns $7,000 of interest income in 1998. As well, your spouse attended university full-time for four months and paid $1,000 in tuition fees. Your spouse would have taxable income of $7,000 and an eligible tuition and education amount of $1,800 [$1,000 + (4 x $200)]. The amount of credits transferable to you is calculated as follows:

Spouse's Tax Liability:

Taxable income	$7,000
	17%
Federal tax (before tax credits)	1,190
Personal tax credit	1,098
Supplementary personal tax credit	
{17% x $500 − [4% x ($7,000 - $6,956)]}/2	42
Federal tax (before tuition credit)	50
Tuition needed to reduce taxes payable to zero	(50)
Federal tax	0

As shown above, your spouse must use a portion of the tuition and education credit in order to eliminate his or her federal tax liability. The remaining tuition and education amount of $1,506 [$1,800-($50/17%)] is eligible for transfer to your 1998 tax return.

65. PENSION CREDIT

There is a tax credit on up to $1,000 of pension income. The amounts eligible for the pension income credit differ depending on whether you were 65 or older in the year. For those under 65 years of age as of December 31, 1998, "qualifying pension income" includes life annuity payments out of a superannuation or pension plan, and certain payments received as a result of the death of a spouse.

If you were 65 or older in 1998, other defined payments such as annuity payments out of your RRSP or RRIF also qualify for the pension credit. Qualifying pension income does not include CPP, Old Age Security (OAS) or guaranteed income supplement (GIS) payments.

U.S. benefits taxed again

Following ratification of a recent protocol to the Canada-U.S. tax treaty, amounts received as retirement or survivor benefits under the U.S. Social Security Act are now subject to tax in Canada again **(see article 83)**. However, only 85% of the amounts received are required to be included in taxable income. Currently, Revenue Canada is allowing this income to qualify for the pension credit; however, this is subject to change. Your tax adviser will be able to provide any clarification you need.

> ▶ *TAX TIP*
> If you do not already benefit from the pension income tax credit, and you are 65 years of age or over, consider creating pension income by purchasing an annuity that yields $1,000 of interest income annually. Alternatively, you can use some of the funds in your RRSP to purchase an annuity or RRIF to provide you with $1,000 of annual pension income.

66. CLAIMS FOR DEPENDANTS

Claims for dependent persons are made through the non-refundable tax credit system. Personal exemption credits are calculated as 17% of specified "personal amounts" **(see Table 1)**, and are allowed as a deduction in computing your federal tax liability.

You may claim personal exemption credits for yourself, your spouse and for certain other persons who are related to you by blood, marriage or adoption. Income earned by your spouse or other dependants may reduce the amount you are entitled to claim. With the exception of the equivalent-to-married credit, a general dependent tax credit cannot be claimed for children under age 19.

The married credit

You may claim a credit for the married amount if, at any time in the year, you were married or had a common-law spouse, you supported your spouse, and you were not living separate and apart because of a breakdown of the marriage.

The equivalent-to-married credit

If at any time during the year you were unmarried or separated from your spouse, you may be entitled to claim a personal tax credit known as the equivalent-to-married credit. To qualify, you must have maintained a home in which you and your qualifying dependant lived. As well, your dependant must be related to you and dependant on you for support. Other qualifying factors include that the dependant is either under 18 years of age at any time during 1998, your parent or grandparent, or mentally or physically infirm. Two or more supporting relatives cannot split this tax credit.

The infirm-dependant credit

Claiming a dependant tax credit for a relative who is 18 years of age or older before the end of the year is allowed, providing that individual is dependent on you because of mental or physical infirmity. In addition, the individual must be dependent on you for support at any time in the year. Unlike the credits above, it is not necessary that the dependant live in the same residence as you.

Supplementary personal credit

The 1998 federal budget proposed the introduction of a non-refundable supplement to the basic personal, married and equivalent-to-married credits (see Table 1). That means individuals will be entitled to a $500 (tax credit of $85) supplement, subject to a reduction when income exceeds $6,956. For a single individual the supplement will be reduced to zero when income exceeds $19,456.

Individuals with a dependant eligible for the married or equivalent-to-married credit may claim an additional supplement in respect of the dependant, provided the dependant's income is not in excess of $6,956.

Again, the total supplement claimed by the individual will be subject to reduction based on the income of the individual and that of the dependant. If the dependant's income exceeds $6,956, the dependant must file a return to claim the supplementary personal amount. This credit came into effect in July 1998, so the credit available for the 1998 taxation year will be only one-half the amount otherwise available.

67. DISABILITY CREDIT

Individuals suffering from severe and prolonged mental or physical impairment can obtain an additional federal credit of $720. To qualify, a doctor must certify on form T2201 that there exists a severe and prolonged impairment that "markedly restricts" the individual's activities of daily living. The impairment must have lasted, or can reasonably be expected to last, for a continuous period of 12 months. Once obtained, the form continues to be valid until the cessation date noted on the form, or until there is a change in condition. There is no requirement to file a new certificate each year.

Beginning with the 1996 taxation year, those making a new application for this credit will find that Revenue Canada will review the claim to determine eligibility before assessing the tax return. Once approved, this amount will be able to be claimed as long as circumstances do not change.

Transferring the credit

If you can't take advantage of this credit, it can be transferred to your spouse or other supporting person. However, no claim may be made under this provision if a medical expense credit has been claimed by you or anyone on your behalf for costs relating to a full-time attendant or nursing home care. On the other hand, you may claim the attendant care deduction (see article 62) and the disability credit at the same time, as long as no additional attendant or nursing home claim has been made on your behalf.

▶ *TAX TIP*

If you or anyone else paid for an attendant or for care in a nursing home or other establishment because of your impairment, it may be beneficial to claim the amounts paid as medical expenses instead of the disability amount. In some circumstances, both may be claimed.

The rules relating to this area of credits are exceedingly complex and often confusing. Before filing a return it is recommended that you have a tax adviser analyze your particular circumstances to come up with the appropriate claim or combination of claims that make sound economic sense.

68. TAX CREDIT FOR CAREGIVERS

Proposed by the 1998 federal budget and effective for 1998 and subsequent years, there is a new tax credit available to individuals who reside with and provide in-home care for a parent or grandparent who is 65 years of age or over. This also applies if the taxpayer has a relative who is dependent by reason of mental or physical infirmity.

Revenue Canada views a person as being infirm if the person is incapable of being gainfully employed for a considerable period of time due to the infirmity. The maximum credit will reduce federal taxes by $400.

If the dependant's income exceeds $11,500, the credit will be reduced. No credit will be available if the dependant's income exceeds $13, 853. And no credit will be available if an equivalent-to-married tax credit or dependant tax credit is claimed in respect of the dependant by any person **(see article 66).**

69. AGE CREDIT

Canadian taxpayers 65 years of age or older are entitled to a tax credit of $592, calculated as 17% of the "age amount," currently at the $3,482 level. With a corresponding reduction in federal surtax and provincial tax, this credit is now worth approximately $950. It is also one of those versatile credits that can be transferred between spouses **(see article 64).**

It is reduced at a rate of 15% to the extent a taxpayer's income exceeds a prescribed threshold amount, currently at $25,921, and it is fully eliminated once income exceeds $49,134.

> ▶ *TAX TIP*
> Are you able to manage your income level, but require over $25,921 per year on average? Then you may find it beneficial to receive larger amounts of income in one year and a reduced amount the next. This will ensure that

the age credit amount is reduced in only one year. Similarly, this strategy may reduce the total Old Age Security clawback **(see article 54)**.

70. CHILD BENEFIT SYSTEM

It's been several years now since the family allowance, the non-refundable tax credit for children under age 18 and the refundable child tax credit were all replaced by the "child tax benefit system." The current child tax benefit system includes a "working income supplement." And now the government is poised to make changes again.

How it works

A monthly payment is issued to those who qualify, and each payment is based on the prior year's combined income of you and your spouse. Payments for the first six months of the year are based on net income from two years ago, and payments for the next six months are based on net income from last year. The monthly benefit is reduced if your combined incomes exceed $25,921, while the working income supplement portion of the payment is reduced if your combined income exceeds $20,921. The payments under this system are not taxable.

What's in store

But come July 1998, as announced in the 1997 federal budget, this current child tax benefit and working income supplement will be replaced by an enriched and simplified program — the Canada Child Tax Benefit (CCTB). The new system will have two major components: the CCTB basic benefit and the CCTB National Child Benefit Supplement. Monthly payments will be structured as outlined above and the same income thresholds will apply — the CCTB basic benefit will be reduced if combined incomes exceed $25,921 and the supplement will be reduced if the combined incomes exceed $20,921. The monthly payments under this system will also not be subject to tax.

▶ **TAX TIP**
To qualify for this new program and receive child benefit payments, you and your spouse must each file an income tax return.

71. TAXATION OF COMMON-LAW COUPLES

The Income Tax Act was amended in 1993 to treat common-law couples the same as legally married couples for all provisions of the Act. A common-law spouse is defined as a person of the opposite sex who has lived with you in a conjugal relationship for at least one year or who is the natural or adoptive parent of your child. As a result, common-law couples are:

- able to claim the married credit
- permitted to contribute to spousal RRSPs
- required to combine their incomes to determine entitlement to the GST credit and the child tax benefit
- subject to the income attribution rules
- allowed to transfer assets to a surviving spouse on a tax-deferred basis upon the death of the other spouse
- subject to all other provisions that formerly applied only to married persons

72. PRINCIPAL RESIDENCE RULES

Your "principal residence" is generally any residential property owned and occupied by you or your spouse, your former spouse or your child at any time in the year. It can be a house, condominium, cottage, mobile home, trailer or even a live-aboard boat, and it need not be located in Canada. Any gain on the sale of a principal residence is tax-free. However, if you sell your principal residence, you should be aware that some tax rules apply.

Just because you live in a house that you own does not automatically qualify it as a principal residence. For example, building contractors or house renovators who follow a pattern of living for a short period of time in a home that they have built or renovated and then selling it at a profit may be subject to tax on their gains as ordinary business income.

Designating a principal residence

A home can be designated as your principal residence for each year in which you, your spouse and/or your children were residents in Canada and ordinarily lived in it for some time during the particular year. You are only allowed to designate one home as your principal residence for a particular year. If you are unable to designate your home as your principal residence for all the years you owned it, a portion of any gain on sale may be subject to tax as a capital gain. The portion of the gain subject to tax is based upon a formula that takes into account the number of years you owned the home and the number of years it was designated as your principal residence.

Suppose you and your spouse own two residences, perhaps a home in the city and a cottage out of town. Only one of these homes can be designated as your family's principal residence each year. Before 1982, each spouse could designate a separate property as a principal residence for a particular year, provided the property was not jointly owned. However, for each year after 1981 the rules have tightened up, and couples cannot designate more than one home in total as their principal residence each year.

To help you make this designation, you should determine the fair market value of both homes as of December 31, 1981. Factors to consider will include the relative appreciation of each house and the expected timing of any sale.

Tax issues

If you made a capital gains election on property designated as a principal residence (see article 92), the tax implications on the eventual disposition of the property will depend on a number of factors. They include the value of the property at the time of disposition, the number of years it was designated as a principal residence at the time of making the capital gains election, and the years it is designated as a principal residence after 1994. A property may still be designated as a principal residence on disposition even if it was not designated as such at the time of making the election. The benefit of the election may, however, be reduced. The rules in this area are quite complex and well worth a trip to your tax adviser's office.

▶ **TAX TIP**
Be careful before designating a foreign-owned home as your principal residence. Even though the gain under Canadian rules is tax-free, you may incur a foreign tax liability when you sell your home.

Homes for rent

If you move out and rent your home, you can continue to treat the house as your principal residence for four additional years, or possibly more. There are also rules that apply if you own property to earn rental income and subsequently convert the property to personal use. Basically, at the time of the change in use, you are deemed to have disposed of the property at its fair market value. If this value exceeds your original cost, you will have to report a capital gain. However, you can make a special election to defer recognizing this gain until you ultimately sell the home. This election is not available if you have claimed depreciation on the property for any year after 1984.

▶ TAX TIP

Contemplating renting out your home or converting a rental property to personal use? Another good reason to visit your tax adviser's office.

73. SELLING PERSONAL-USE CAPITAL PROPERTY

Profits from the sale of almost all capital assets, with the exception of your principal residence, are subject to tax as a capital gain. Unfortunately, losses from the sale of most personal capital assets are not deductible.

What's involved

If you sell your boat or car at a loss, you cannot claim it as a capital loss. But if you sell it at a profit, three-quarters of the gain is taxable. Assets that have a cost of $1,000 or less and are sold for $1,000 or less are exempt from this rule. But don't start preparing that For Sale ad just yet — assets that cost less than $1,000 but are sold for more than $1,000 still face a tax bill on the difference between their sale price and the $1,000 cut-off point.

When a capital gains election was made on a personal-use property **(see article 92)**, the cost base of the asset generally is the amount designated in the election. When the asset is sold, the difference between the sale price and the amount elected is a capital gain.

Losses from the sale of certain types of personal property, referred to as "listed personal property," can be applied against gains from the sale of such property. Listed personal property includes coins, stamps, jewellery, rare books, paintings or sculptures, and other similar works of art. Listed personal-property losses can be carried back three years and forward seven years, but they can only be applied against gains from the sale of similar property.

EXAMPLE

Buying and selling

In 1996 you purchased a painting (which is listed personal property) at a cost of $2,000, and a boat (which is personal-use property) at a cost of $3,500. Two years later in 1998, you sold both items for $3,000 each. The sale of the painting will result in a capital gain of $1,000 ($3,000 - $2,000) to be reported on your 1998 tax return. The sale of the boat triggered a capital loss of $500 ($3,000 - $3,500), which cannot be claimed because it is personal-use property and not listed personal property.

However, if the asset in question was a diamond necklace instead of a boat (assuming the same cost and sale price), the capital loss may be applied against the gain on the painting resulting in a net capital gain of $500 being reported on your 1998 tax return.

74. TRANSFERS/LOANS TO SPOUSES AND FAMILY MEMBERS

All capital properties, such as shares in companies and real estate, are automatically transferred between spouses on a tax-free basis. If you want the transfer to take place at fair market value, you must file a special election requesting this treatment when you file your tax return for the year of the transfer. If such an election is filed, you will report a capital gain (assuming the property has appreciated in value) and the tax cost of the property to your spouse will increase accordingly.

Selling the property

When the property is eventually sold by your spouse to a third party, you will have to report any capital gain realized on the sale unless the following very specific requirements have been met. These include fair market value being paid for the property at the time of the transfer. You must also have made the fair market value election (as noted above), and sufficient annual interest on any unpaid purchase price must have been paid in full no later than January 30 of the following year. Provided these conditions have been met, any subsequent capital gain realized on a sale to a third party will be taxed in your spouse's hands.

EXAMPLE

Sharing the wealth

A benevolent mood comes over you and you decide to transfer your shares of XYZ Co. to your spouse. You acquired the shares in 1994 at a cost of $1,000 and they have a current fair market value of $5,000. For tax purposes, your spouse will be deemed to have acquired the shares from you at a cost of $1,000. Therefore, you will not recognize a capital gain or loss on the transfer. However, you will be taxed on any capital gain arising when your spouse disposes of the shares. The capital gain will be calculated using your original cost amount of $1,000.

Alternatively, you may elect, by attaching a note to your tax return, to have the transfer take place at fair market value. As a result of making this election, you will report a capital gain of $4,000 and your spouse will be deemed to have acquired the shares from you at a cost of $5,000.

Now assume you have made this election and your spouse subsequently sells the shares for $6,000. If your spouse did not pay you fair market value for the shares, the resulting capital gain of $1,000 is taxable in your hands. However, if your spouse paid you $5,000 for the shares, say by way of a loan from you, the $1,000 gain would be taxable in your spouse's hands — that is, provided your spouse pays a reasonable rate of annual interest on the loan within the required time period.

Special rules apply where the property has been transferred between spouses, or common-law spouses, as part of a property settlement or where the couple is separated at the time of sale to a third party.

A transfer of capital property to other family members is taxed just as if you sold the property at its fair market value. If the property has been transferred to a child, grandchild, niece or nephew, you must report any income earned on such property until the child reaches 18 years of age. After 18, that individual must report the income.

▶ **TAX TIP**
> Unless the person receiving the property is your spouse, there is no require-
> ment to attribute capital gains to you, the transferor. Consider buying capi-
> tal property (such as equity-based mutual funds) with a low yield but high
> capital gains potential in the names of your children. The income will be
> attributed to you, but any future capital gains will be taxed in your children's
> hands.

Low-interest and interest-free loans

Caution should be exercised if you provide low-interest or interest-free
loans to family members to either enable them to purchase income-
producing assets or as consideration for the transfer of assets. If one of
the main reasons for the loan is to reduce or avoid tax, you must report
any income earned on the property regardless of the age of the recipient of the loan. An outright gift to a child, or anyone other than a
spouse who is 18 years or older, is not subject to this rule.

▶ **TAX TIP**
> Any involvement in the transfer of property or the lending of money to a
> spouse or other family members should have you consulting your tax advis-
> er to ensure that the tax consequences of such transactions do not create a
> greater tax burden.

75. REGISTERED EDUCATION SAVINGS PLANS (RESPs)

An RESP is a type of trust through which you can save for a child's education. If the child does not pursue an education, the principal you contributed to the RESP is returned, but you may forfeit all of the earnings. Those earnings are then shared among other students in the plan
who are pursuing a post-secondary education.

Contributions to the plan are not tax-deductible, but the major
advantage of such a plan is that earnings accumulate on a tax-deferred
basis. When the funds are finally issued to the child, only the interest
portion is considered the child's income and taxed at his or her lower
rate.

Important changes

Beginning in 1997, the federal budget increased the annual contribution limit to $4,000 per beneficiary from the 1996 limit of $2,000. The
lifetime limit remains at $42,000 per beneficiary. Several plans include

a transferability feature. What this does is allow you to change the beneficiary of the plan to someone else or to even sell the plan should you conclude the designated child has no interest in post-secondary education.

To encourage use of RESPs and minimize the risk of forfeited investment income, the 1997 federal budget introduced changes that allow contributors to receive RESP income directly, under certain circumstances. So if after 1997 you have made contributions to an RESP — which has existed for at least 10 years and none of the intended beneficiaries are pursuing a higher education by the age of 21 — you will be allowed to receive the RESP income and you may be allowed to transfer it to your RRSP (or your spouse's RRSP). Of course this is based on the proviso that you have sufficient RRSP room to claim an RRSP deduction for the year of the transfer.

The total RESP income that you may transfer to an RRSP is subject to a lifetime limit of $40,000. However, the 1998 federal budget has proposed that this amount be raised to $50,000 for 1999 and subsequent years. If the RESP income is not fully offset by RRSP deductions, the excess will be subject to a 20% penalty in addition to regular taxes.

The benefits of RESPs must be weighed carefully, not simply in tax terms, but with an understanding of the future costs of post-secondary education, not to mention plan provisions in the event that beneficiaries do not ultimately attend designated schools within the anticipated time frame.

More incentives introduced
And the government hasn't slowed down its revamping of these plans just yet. With the 1998 federal budget, the government has proposed a system of grants designed to help the RESP to earn income at a faster rate. That should make these types of plans a somewhat more attractive vehicle by which to save for family members' post-secondary education.

Canada Education Savings Grant (CESG)
Beginning in 1998, the government will provide, through the Canada Education Savings Grant program, a sum equal to 20% of the first $2,000 of annual contributions to an RESP (up to $400 per year per child) for the benefit of children up to age 18. The grant will be paid

directly to the RESP and will not exceed $7,200 for any one beneficiary.

For example, you set up an RESP for your toddler and make a $3,000 contribution during 1998. A CESG of $400 (i.e., 20% of $2,000) will be paid to the plan trustee. This amount, together with the accumulating investment income and contributions, will be available for educational assistance payments made out of the RESP.

When RESP funds are paid to a beneficiary, a formula will determine what portion of each payment is considered to be a distribution of the CESG. No single beneficiary may receive more than $7,200 of CESG from the plan.

If the contributor does not make a contribution to the RESP in one or more years, there are carry-forward provisions that can increase the CESG maximum from $400 to $800.

The grant is available for beneficiaries aged 17 and under in the year, and there are no restrictions for beneficiaries aged 15 and under in the year. RESP contributions for children aged 16 and 17 in a particular year will be eligible for a grant only if there have been contributions made for the child for at least four years, or if the previous contributions were at least $4,000. This means that a new plan will not get the CESG for a beneficiary who is 16 or 17. These age restrictions are in place to encourage early RESP savings.

An RESP will be required to repay CESG money in certain situations, such as if a beneficiary does not pursue higher education or if the plan is terminated.

As cited above, in the event that beneficiaries do not, in fact, undertake post-secondary education, contributions may be returned to the contributor without tax. The income element of the amounts returned will be included in the contributor's income. The contributor may transfer the RESP investment income (which may include investment income earned on the CESG) into an RRSP, subject to the limits discussed. The investment income in excess of that transferred to an RRSP will be subjected to the 20% penalty tax in addition to regular income tax.

Some of the above information is based on proposed legislation. The rules may change before the law is enacted.

76. SPLITTING CPP BENEFITS WITH SPOUSE

The Canada Pension Plan Act permits you to assign a portion of your retirement pension to your spouse. In many cases the assignment of benefits allows you and your spouse to equalize CPP retirement benefits.

Suppose you are entitled to $6,000 in annual CPP benefits, but your spouse is entitled to only $1,200. This assignment will generally result in each of you receiving $3,600 annually. If your spouse is in a lower tax bracket than you, shifting this income to his or her hands helps lower the total family tax bill **(see article 77)**. The number of months you and your spouse have lived together is a factor in determining how the benefits are split.

If you both receive a CPP retirement pension, the assignment must be made for both retirement pensions. But if only one of you receives a retirement pension, the assignment can only be made if the other spouse has reached 60 years of age and is not a contributor to the CPP.

Divorced and separated couples

Although an assignment generally ceases on divorce, there are rules to permit you to apply for a share of the CPP credits of your former spouse if you were divorced after January 1, 1978. Also, CPP benefits can be split on the breakdown of a common-law relationship provided you have lived together for at least one year and application is made within four years of the commencement of the separation. You can obtain application forms from your local Human Resources Development Canada office.

77. INCOME SPLITTING WITH FAMILY MEMBERS

Income splitting is a tax-planning technique designed to shift income from a taxpayer paying tax at a high rate to another taxpayer within the family unit paying tax at a lower rate. Unfortunately, there are a number of legislative provisions — "attribution rules" — designed to prevent tax savings by shifting income between taxpayers **(see article 74)**.

Arrangements that are permitted

There are still a number of legitimate tax-planning arrangements that can be used to effectively redistribute income in a family unit. These include:

- having your business pay a reasonable salary to your spouse or children **(see article 8)**
- making contributions to a spousal RRSP **(see articles 41-43)**
- investing child benefit system payments in your child's name **(see article 70)**
- sharing CPP payments with your spouse **(see article 76)**
- having the higher-income spouse assume most or all of the personal household expenses, leaving the lower-income spouse with as much disposable income as possible to invest
- transferring or selling assets to family members for fair market value consideration **(see article 74)**
- taking advantage of the fact that income earned on income is not subject to the attribution rules — although the initial income earned on property loaned to a non-arm's-length person may be attributed back to the person making the transfer, income earned on that income will not be attributed

EXAMPLE

Bypassing attribution

If you purchased $1,000 in 5% bonds on behalf of your 10-year-old son in 1997, he would receive $50 of interest on the bond in 1998. At that time, he turns around and invests the interest in additional 5% bonds. In 1999, your son will again receive interest of $50 on the original bonds, plus $2.50 on the bonds purchased in 1998. Although the $50 received by your son in both years is taxable in your hands, he reports the $2.50 received in 1999.

- using a management company — however, if the management company provides services to a professional who provides tax-exempt services under the GST, the taxable GST charge will pre-

sent an absolute increase in cost that may outweigh the income-splitting benefits of the management company
- creating testamentary trusts in your will to split income
- contributing to an RESP **(see article 75)**
- giving cash or other assets to your adult children **(see article 74)**
- having your spouse and/or children participate in an incorporated business by owning shares acquired with their own funds — this would allow company profits to be distributed to your spouse and/or children in the form of dividends

It's crucial that you confer with your tax adviser who can review your personal situation and advise you which income-splitting strategies best fit your circumstances.

78. SOCIAL INSURANCE NUMBERS AND T5 SLIPS

A social insurance number (SIN) is mandatory if you want to file a personal income tax return. You are also required to provide your SIN when requested by third parties that issue T5s (slips that identify interest earned or dividends received), or other information forms that are to accompany your return. If you do not have a number, you are required to apply for one within 15 days of the request.

Avoiding fines

Employers and institutions issuing information slips such as T5s must make a reasonable effort to obtain the SIN for each individual receiving a slip. If you prepare the information slip, you are liable for a penalty of $100 for each slip in which the SIN has been omitted unless you have made a reasonable effort to obtain it. Similarly, if you are requested to provide your SIN, you are liable for a penalty of $100 for each failure to provide the number within a reasonable period of time — unless you apply for the number within 15 days of being requested to provide it. When you receive the number you must provide it to the person requesting it within 15 days. These penalties are designed to put the onus on the institution or individual preparing the information slip.

79. SOME INCOME IS TAX-FREE

Almost all types of income are subject to income tax. No surprise there. But what is surprising is that there are a few exceptions open to you.

If you are lucky enough to win a lottery, the amount you win is not taxable. But any income you receive from investing the money is taxable. Gains from casual gambling are not taxable. Proceeds from damage awards are generally tax-free, and under certain circumstances, income arising from damage awards for taxpayers under 21 years of age is also exempt until the taxpayer is 21. Various defined payments to war veterans are also exempt.

Workers' Compensation Board and welfare payments are also not directly subject to tax. However, they are a factor in determining eligibility for certain tax credits. The amounts must be included when computing net income. To arrive at taxable income, an offsetting deduction is permitted.

80. GIVING UP CANADIAN RESIDENCE

Proposed changes announced in 1996, and expected to be enacted soon, have altered the tax consequences to Canadians leaving Canada. In general, if you cease to be a resident of Canada, you will be deemed to have disposed of, and to have reacquired, all your capital property at its fair market value on that date. You will have to pay tax on any taxable capital gain resulting from this deemed disposition.

Under the proposed changes the deemed disposition rules above apply to all capital property, other than Canadian real estate, Canadian business property, and certain other exclusions such as retirement savings in RRSPs and stock options. These changes apply to individuals leaving Canada after October 1, 1996.

All the implications

Tax triggered on the deemed disposition can either be paid when filing your income tax return or deferred until the property is actually sold. In that case, you must provide acceptable security to Revenue Canada. After you have left Canada there may be further tax to pay. When you dispose of property excluded from the deemed disposition rules, you are required to file a Canadian income tax return and pay tax on any resulting gain. In addition, when you actually dispose of capital property that has been subject to the deemed disposition rules and that is considered "taxable Canadian property" as defined below, you are required to file a Canadian income tax return. Additional Canadian tax may be payable on the gain accruing after you leave Canada.

Under the current law, the deemed disposition rules apply to all capital property other than "taxable Canadian property." Taxable Canadian property includes real property located in Canada, such as land and buildings, capital property used in carrying on business in Canada, shares of a private corporation resident in Canada, and certain shares of public corporations. Currently, you are not deemed to have disposed of such property when you leave Canada. However, when you do dispose of it, you are required to file a Canadian income tax return and pay tax on any resulting gain.

Reporting requirement

In addition to expanding the types of properties subject to the deemed disposition rules, the 1996 proposals introduced a reporting requirement for individuals leaving Canada after 1995. You will now be required to report your property holdings to Revenue Canada if you own property with a total value of more than $25,000 at the date of departure from Canada.

Exceptions will be provided for personal use property with a value of less than $10,000. If you are subject to this reporting requirement, you must complete form T1161 (which is available only in draft because the rules are not yet law) and attach it to your income tax return for the year of departure.

▶ **TAX TIP**

The capital gains deduction is not available to a non-resident of Canada. If you have shares of a corporation that is a "qualified small business corporation" **(see article 93)**, or have an interest in a farm operation **(see article 94)**, there may be opportunities to utilize the $500,000 capital gains deduction. Review this with your tax adviser, as extensive planning is required.

81. TAKING UP CANADIAN RESIDENCE

Welcome to Canada. For an individual who became a resident of Canada during 1998, there is a special set of income tax rules. For instance, all your capital property, except taxable Canadian property **(see article 80)**, will be deemed to have been acquired by you at its fair market value on the date you take up residence. Any gain or loss on a subsequent disposition of that property will be calculated on its value.

How much tax will you pay?

If you were not employed in Canada and had not carried on a business in Canada before becoming a resident, you are only taxed on your worldwide income from the date you become a resident of Canada. However, if you were employed or carried on a business in Canada prior to becoming a resident, you will also be taxed on your income earned in Canada for that part of the year you were a non-resident of Canada.

You are entitled to claim personal tax credits, but the amounts are generally reduced on a pro rata basis according to the number of days in the year that you are taxed on your worldwide income.

EXAMPLE

What you can claim

Suppose you are single, have no children, and immigrated to Canada on June 1, 1998. During the first part of the year, you were employed in a foreign country. You would be entitled to claim a basic personal amount of $3,785 ($6,456 x 214/365).

If you arrived from a country that has a tax treaty with Canada, any provision in the treaty that conflicts with the Canadian tax rules will override the Canadian rule.

▶ *TAX TIP*

Make sure that you are aware of the exemption from the new foreign reporting rules for the year in which you first become resident in Canada **(see article 109)**.

82. U.S. CITIZENS RESIDENT IN CANADA

The United States taxes its citizens on their worldwide income, whether or not they live in the United States. As a result, if you are a U.S. citizen living in Canada, you are required to file a tax return under both systems.

Watch out for tax liabilities

Although there are several mechanisms in place to prevent double taxation, there are still many differences between the two tax systems that can lead to unexpected tax liabilities. One of the most glaring differences between the two systems is in the area of capital gains. For this reason, you should always obtain professional tax advice if you have sold or are considering selling capital property.

▶ **TAX TIP**

If your income is high enough, you may also have to pay a certain amount of U.S. alternative minimum tax even though your income is fully taxed in Canada. Be aware of this potential liability when planning your income.

Filing your returns

For Canadian tax purposes, each taxpayer must file a separate return. For U.S. tax purposes, you have the option of filing a joint return with your spouse. If your spouse has little or no income but you are paying tax to the United States, filing a joint election will generally be beneficial.

If your spouse is not a U.S. citizen, you can still file a joint return but the rules are a little more complicated. First of all, an election must be filed to treat your non-resident spouse as a U.S. citizen. Once this election is made, your spouse must file a U.S. income tax return each year until the election is revoked. Once revoked, the election cannot be reinstated. During the years in which the election is in force, you and your spouse may decide annually whether to elect to file a joint return. This decision can change from year to year. A discussion with your tax adviser is recommended.

If you are a U.S. citizen, you may be required to file a U.S. tax return even if no U.S. tax is owing. On October 1, 1992, the Internal Revenue Service (IRS) launched a "non-filer program" in an attempt to bring back into the U.S. tax system taxpayers who have not been filing returns. Substantial resources are being devoted to finding non-filers who are likely to owe a significant amount of tax.

An IRS information return must now be completed in conjunction with the processing of all passport applications. If you have not been filing a U.S. return, you should get professional advice. As well as filing a tax return, you may also be required to disclose a substantial amount of other financial information to the U.S. government.

83. U.S. SOCIAL SECURITY PAYMENTS

Taxation of Social Security payments from the United States was changed as of January 1, 1996. And now it has changed again.

A little history

Prior to the most recent changes, U.S. social security payments received after January 1, 1996, were not taxable in Canada. However, the U.S. government withheld tax at a rate of 25.5% on all payments made to non-U.S. citizens who were resident in Canada, and the U.S. tax withheld was not refundable. U.S. citizens who were resident in Canada were exempt from the withholding tax but paid U.S. income tax, if required, upon filing their U.S. income tax return.

What the changes mean

Under the most recent changes, U.S. social security benefits received by residents of Canada will only be subject to tax in Canada. The United States will no longer tax these benefits.

The full amount of the benefit received will be included in net income, but 15% of that amount will be deductible in computing taxable income. As a result, only 85% of the benefits received in a year will be subject to tax. But the full amount is included in net income for purposes of assessing various clawbacks and other net income-based calculations — the OAS clawback **(see article 54)** and the age credit **(see article 69)**. Also, Revenue Canada is currently allowing these benefits to qualify for the pension income credit **(see article 65)**.

These changes are retroactive to January 1, 1996. However, Canadian tax returns for 1996 and 1997 were filed as if the most recent changes had not taken effect. Revenue Canada will apply the changes for the retroactive period — 1996 and 1997 — so that any excess tax paid under the old rule will be refunded. And the good news doesn't end there. If Revenue Canada finds that any additional taxes are owed, you will not be liable for them. That means Revenue Canada will automatically issue refunds for 1996 and 1997 to non-U.S. citizens if the Canadian tax on the benefit would have been less than the U.S. tax withheld. Tax returns for 1998 are to be filed under the new rules.

▶ *TAX TIP*

Did you receive U.S. social security payments in 1996 and/or 1997? If so, and you think that the Canadian tax that would have been payable is less than the U.S. tax withheld on the benefits in those years, and you have not yet received a refund, get your tax adviser working on it.

84. U.S. REAL ESTATE OWNED BY CANADIAN RESIDENTS

For Canadian residents who receive rent from U.S. real estate, a withholding tax of 30% normally applies to the gross amount of any rent paid. As an alternative, you can elect to pay tax on a net income basis. In this case, you must file a U.S. tax return at the end of the year, reporting your net rental income. By making this election with the Internal Revenue Service and providing appropriate information to the tenant, the 30% withholding tax is not required. Once you make this election, it is permanent and can only be revoked in limited circumstances.

Many people assume that because their expenses always exceed their rental income, there is no need to file a U.S. tax return or to have tax withheld at source. However, if tax is not withheld at source, a tax return must be filed within a certain time period if you want to claim expenses.

▶ *TAX TIP*

Professional advice is the best remedy if you receive rental income from U.S. real property and have not filed a U.S. return because your expenses exceed your rental income. The U.S. has strict rules regarding the timely filing of such returns. If the returns are not filed by a specified deadline, you will not be entitled to claim any deductions and tax will be assessed on the gross income.

Selling your U.S. property

Selling your U.S. real property? Then expect to pay 10% withholding tax. However, this withholding will not apply if the property is sold for less than $300,000 (U.S.) and the purchaser intends to use the property as a residence. Also, you can apply to the IRS to have the withholding tax reduced if the expected tax liability on the sale will be less than 10% of the sale price.

Regardless of the amount of withholding tax, the gain on the sale of any U.S. property is still taxable in the United States, and a U.S. tax return must be filed. The U.S. tax that applies generates a foreign tax credit that can be used to reduce the Canadian tax on the sale. If you have owned the property continuously since before September 27, 1980, for personal use only, a provision of the Canada-U.S. tax treaty can be used to reduce the gain.

85. U.S. ESTATE TAX

The estate of a deceased Canadian could be subject to U.S. estate tax on the full value of the deceased's taxable estate located in the United States. Tax is applied on the value of the U.S. property. The major types of assets subject to U.S. estate tax are U.S. real property, shares of U.S. companies, tangible personal property located in the U.S. and debts issued by U.S. residents, including the U.S. government.

However, there is good news — the Canada-U.S. tax treaty may provide significant relief in this area. First, you are not subject to U.S. estate tax if the value of your worldwide gross estate is less than $625,000 (U.S.). This amount will increase to $650,000 for 1999 and will continue to increase gradually to $1 million by the year 2006. Second, if you do not own U.S. real property or certain U.S. business property, your worldwide gross estate must exceed $1,200,000 (U.S.) before you are subject to estate tax. On top of that, Revenue Canada may allow a foreign tax credit for any U.S. estate taxes payable.

▶ *TAX TIP*

Do you own or are you about to acquire property situated in the United States? If so, consult your tax adviser to review your exposure to U.S. federal estate tax. Planning strategies are available to defer, reduce or eliminate this potential liability.

86. U.S. RESIDENCY REGULATIONS

Many Canadians who regularly spend winters in the United States may find that they are required to fill out a special declaration — "Closer

Connection Exemption Statement" — in order to be exempt from paying American taxes.

Are you exempt?

To determine whether you are one of the Canadians who should file this declaration, you must add up the number of days (or part days) you spent in the United States in 1998, one-third of the days in 1997 and one-sixth of the days in 1996. If this calculation adds up to 183 days or more, you may be considered a U.S. resident for tax purposes.

However, you can qualify for the "closer connection" exemption if you meet certain provisions. These include that you have not applied for a U.S. green card; were present in the United States for less than 183 days in 1998; have maintained a permanent place of residence in Canada throughout 1998; can claim a closer connection to Canada; and file the special declaration by June 15, 1999.

Green card holders are not entitled to file this declaration. If you hold a green card or if you spent more than 182 days in the United States in the current year, you will have to rely on the tie-breaker rules in the Canada-U.S. treaty to avoid U.S. resident status. As a cautionary note, U.S. Immigration has issued a warning to green card holders that they may jeopardize their green card status if they use treaty provisions to be taxed as a non-resident of the United States.

> ▶ *TAX TIP*
> Over the past several years, the United States has issued numerous rules and regulations of concern to Canadians with interests in that country. If you spend a considerable amount of time in the United States each year, contact your tax adviser to ensure that you are complying with these rules.

87. ESTATE PLANNING

Estate planning is a difficult subject to deal with briefly. It is not possible to advise people on matters of estate planning without considerable reference to other areas of taxation and to personal and financial objectives.

An ongoing process, estate planning means different things to different people. However, estate planning primarily means the arranging of your financial affairs during your lifetime in such a manner that income taxes and estate administration fees are minimized upon death, and any income tax liability is properly provided for.

Estate planning can include such things as:

- transferring assets to family members during one's lifetime
- capping the value of growth assets at their current values by transferring future asset appreciation to other family members (estate freezing)
- charitable giving
- preparation of a will
- acquisition of life insurance if needed to fund an income tax liability

Asset transfers

If you have decided that you have more assets than you or your spouse needs, you can reduce your estate probate fees and executor fees, and possibly income taxes upon death. What you have to do is transfer assets to your children or other family members during your lifetime. However, if these assets have increased in value since acquisition, the transfer could cause an income tax liability. Appropriate action would be to assess which assets to transfer and how to avoid triggering a tax hit.

▶ TAX TIP
Consider gifting non-growth assets, or those that have not yet increased in value, to your children during your lifetime.

Freezing your estate

Estate freezing is a popular method of limiting death taxes. It primarily consists of transferring the growth potential of assets, such as real estate or shares of corporations, to a younger generation. By doing so, the asset value to the transferor is frozen at the value at the date of transfer. Accordingly, the amount of potential capital gain on death is also frozen. One can better plan for the payment of income taxes on death if one can reasonably estimate the amount of potential taxes, as would be the case if the capital gain is frozen.

You can usually accomplish estate freezing through a transfer of assets to a corporation. The mechanics can vary, but the transfer must be professionally planned in order to avoid running afoul of the many punitive provisions of the Income Tax Act.

▶ *TAX TIP*

For those fortunate enough to have assets that can provide an income larger than lifetime needs, gifting some of the assets to beneficiaries during your lifetime is a logical way to reduce taxes. Complicated rules exist regarding income and capital gains on gifts to spouses and children under 18 years of age **(see article 74)**.

Charitable giving

The value of your estate can be reduced by making charitable donations during your lifetime. The added benefit is that you also earn income tax credits during your life rather than for your estate. New income tax rules have made charitable giving extremely tax effective. Credits can be obtained on donations up to 75% of your net income or more in certain circumstances **(see article 59)**.

▶ *TAX TIP*

Planning to make significant charitable donations through your estate? It may not be your best option. If you make them during your lifetime, you will reduce the value of your estate for probate purposes, reduce your executor fees, and get tax savings earlier.

Preparing a will

On death, you are deemed to have disposed of all capital property at fair market value, with the exception of property passing to a spouse or to certain trusts created for the benefit of a spouse. This deemed disposition can create a very large income tax bill unless your will provides for the disposition of the affected properties directly to your spouse or to a spousal trust.

Both you and your spouse should have wills. This is probably one of the most critical elements of your estate-planning strategy, as dying intestate (without a will) can defeat almost all the estate-planning arrangements you have put into place.

▶ *TAX TIP*

A periodic review of your will is part of prudent estate planning. It should be done to ensure that your assets will be dealt with in the most tax-effective manner and that your will complies with current laws, such as provincial family law acts.

Life insurance

Sometimes, just as you can't avoid death, it is also not possible to avoid taxes when you die. If your estate has sufficient liquid assets, the payment of income taxes may not be much of a problem for your estate. But, if a major portion of your estate consists of shares of private companies or real estate, it may not be possible to satisfy your tax bill on death, at least not without selling off the assets.

The funding of potential income taxes through the purchase of life insurance is often a most effective estate-planning tool. If sufficient insurance proceeds are available, any income tax arising on the deemed dispositions of assets on your death can be paid without resorting to the sale of your assets. Having to sell off the assets means, of course, they cannot be passed on to beneficiaries.

▶ *TAX TIP*

You have made the decision to acquire life insurance to fund any income taxes that may arise from the deemed disposition of shares of a private corporation. Careful planning should be undertaken to determine whether you should be the owner of the policy rather than your company. Both options have different advantages. A consultation with your tax and insurance advisers is a must.

In This Section

Investors

B y your very nature, being an investor means that you will earn money. And, when you earn money, the tax collector is never far behind. In this section there are almost two dozen items that outline what you can do and can't do — with regard to tax relief as you put your money to work.

Items discussed include rental properties, all and sundry regarding capital gains and the capital gains deduction, business investment losses, and capital loss rules. Investment vehicles such as Canada Savings Bonds and mutual funds are examined, and taxation of interest and dividend income is fully explained, as is the deductibility of interest expense.

The use of the resource sector as a tax shelter is addressed, as are limited partnerships. If you have earned investment income from foreign sources, you can find out what your tax obligations are in that respect; as well, you can learn more about the new foreign reporting requirements. Also included is the most recent information on the alternative minimum tax.

To round out the section, numerous tax tips illuminate some of the strategies you can and should use to your advantage as you build your portfolio.

88. RENTAL PROPERTIES

If you owned a rental property in 1998, any net income or loss must be reported on your 1998 income tax return. Rental income is usually reported on a calendar-year basis because the earnings are classified as property income and not as business income. Any income or loss from a rental property you own outside of Canada must also be included in your return.

What can I deduct?

All reasonable expenses incurred in operating the property can be deducted. This can include the cost of insurance, property taxes, mortgage interest, power supply, heat, repairs and even advertising for tenants. If you borrowed money to make the down payment on the rental property, interest on that loan is also deductible. In certain circumstances, you may also be able to claim depreciation.

> ▶ *TAX TIP*
> Keep accurate records of all expenses relating to your rental property. Retain all receipts – make a small note on each one pointing out what the money was spent on and why. It will help your adviser quickly determine if it's a valid expense and eligible for deduction or depreciation.

What can I depreciate?

In general, depreciation on a rental property cannot be used to either create or increase your rental loss. This restriction also applies to certain multiple-unit residential properties (MURBs), which were excepted from this rule in years prior to 1994. When more than one rental property is owned, all of the rental income is combined to determine the total income or loss for the year.

Depreciation may only be claimed on the property to the extent of any net income from the rental of these properties before depreciation. Net income for purposes of determining the amount of depreciation that may be claimed includes recaptured depreciation on another rental property.

> ▶ *TAX TIP*
> If capital costs are required, try to time them for the end of the year instead of the first of the following year. This will speed up your tax depreciation

expense – in other words, you will be able to depreciate it immediately instead of having to wait another 12 months.

What happens if I sell?

Two different types of income may arise on the sale of your rental property. If you sell your property for more than its original cost, you have to report a capital gain. If the property was purchased before February 1992, some or all of this gain may have been eligible for the capital gains deduction. To take advantage of this, however, you should have made a special election on filing your 1994 return **(see article 92)**.

What else should I be aware of?

You may also have to pay tax on income that represents previously claimed depreciation. If proceeds from the sale exceed the undepreciated capital cost (UCC) of the property, the excess, up to the original cost, is taxed as recaptured depreciation in the year of sale.

If the proceeds are more than the original cost, there will be a full recapture and a capital gain. And if the proceeds are less than the original cost, but greater than the UCC, there will be no capital gain and the recapture will be measured as the difference between the proceeds and the UCC. In some cases, where the property was destroyed or expropriated, and another property was purchased, the gain and/or recapture may be deferred.

EXAMPLE

The UCC factor

You purchased a building in 1990 at a cost of $100,000 and the UCC at the end of 1997 was $80,000. If you sell the building in 1998 for proceeds of $110,000, you will have to report recapture of $20,000 and a capital gain of $10,000. If you sell the building for $90,000, you will have to report recapture of $10,000 and there is no capital gain to report.

Anything else?

You may have a terminal loss if the proceeds of the sale are less than the UCC of the property, and this loss is deductible from your other sources of income. In the past, Revenue Canada often disallowed such losses on the basis that the taxpayer had "no reasonable expectation of profit." However, in a 1996 court case, the presiding judge found that this test should be used sparingly where it is evident that a loss does not have a personal or non-business motive. The same applies in determining whether rental losses should be deductible.

Also, if you did not receive the full proceeds of the sale in the year of the sale, you may be able to claim a reserve for capital gain **(see article 95)**. However, you cannot claim any reserve against the recaptured depreciation.

89. TERMINAL LOSS RESTRICTIONS

When you sell a building at a loss, certain rules may reduce the loss for tax purposes. If the building was sold together with the underlying land, the transaction is treated as if you sold two separate items. If the portion of the sale price attributed to the building is less than its undepreciated cost, you may be required to increase the portion allocated to the building and reduce the portion allocated to the land. This will result in a reduced terminal loss on the building.

These rules only apply to depreciable buildings and do not apply to a real estate developer who is holding real estate as inventory.

90. JOINT OWNER OR PARTNER?

If you acquired a partial interest in a rental property, it is important to know whether it is in a partnership or in a joint venture. If you do not know which it is, consult your tax adviser.

With an interest in a partnership, you must report your share of its net profit or loss on your personal tax return. Depreciation is computed at the partnership level, not by each individual partner.

As a joint owner, you have to report your share of the revenue and expenses related to the property. Next, you compute depreciation based upon the cost of your share of the property. Your depreciation claim is independent of the depreciation that may be claimed by the other joint owners.

▶ *TAX TIP*
Where rental properties are owned in a partnership and outside a partnership, a reorganization of ownership may allow increased depreciation charges. Consult your tax adviser on the merits of restructuring.

GST reporting

Reporting requirements under the GST also differ, depending on ownership status. If the property is held as a partnership, the partnership determines whether it is required to register. If the partnership registers, GST returns are filed by the partnership, not the individual partners. If the property is held as a joint venture, the individual members are required to register and file GST returns. In certain cases, an election is available to allow one member of the joint venture to file on behalf of any or all of the members.

91. WHAT ABOUT CAPITAL GAINS?

A capital gain occurs when you sell a capital property for more than its original cost. When you realize a capital gain, the taxable portion is calculated as three-quarters of the gain and added to your other income for the year. In essence, one-quarter of the gain is not subject to tax.

When is a gain a capital gain?

In most circumstances, there is no set rule that determines whether a particular gain should be treated as a capital gain. Most individuals who invest in the stock market can treat their gains and losses as capital gains or losses. However, if you spend considerable time playing the market and/or borrow money to make your purchases, your profits or losses may be taxed in full as business income.

Similarly, if you bought a property intentionally to resell at a profit, the entire gain would be taxable (rather than just three-quarters). For example, taxpayers who purchase property for immediate resale, called "flipping," are subject to tax on the full gain, even though they may have spent little time on the venture and may have sold only one or two properties. In some cases there is no clear-cut answer. If in doubt, consult your tax adviser.

▶ *TAX TIP*

Most taxpayers are eligible to elect capital gains treatment from the disposition of qualifying Canadian securities by filing form T123. However, once you make the election, all subsequent gains and losses from the disposition of qualifying securities will be recorded as capital gains and losses. Be sure you understand the implications of making this election before you file the form.

92. LIFETIME CAPITAL GAINS DEDUCTION

In 1985, every Canadian became eligible for a limited lifetime capital gains deduction. Virtually every year since then, more and more restrictions have been placed on the availability of the deduction. In 1994, it was eliminated for dispositions of property after February 22, 1994, other than shares of qualified small business corporations **(see article 93)** and qualified farm property **(see article 94).**

$100,000 capital gains deduction

Other property having an accrued gain on February 22, 1994, was eligible for the $100,000 capital gains deduction, if you made a special one-time-only election "capital gains election." In most cases, this election had to be made on your 1994 tax return. The election allowed you to opt to have a deemed disposition of any capital property you owned on February 22, 1994, at any amount up to its fair market value on that day.

Depending on the type of capital property, the amount you elected as a deemed disposition became your new cost base. Or, in some cases, the gain created a special tax account which may be used to reduce a gain on that property in later years **(see articles 26 and 102)**. The election was made by filing form T664 with your income tax return.

▶ *TAX TIP*

If you still own property for which a capital gains election was made, you should continue to monitor the revised cost base to ensure it is taken into consideration upon a subsequent sale of the property.

93. QUALIFIED SMALL BUSINESS CORPORATIONS CAPITAL GAINS DEDUCTION

Shares of a qualified small business corporation (QSBC) continue to qualify for an enhanced $500,000 capital gain deduction. However, a study completed and presented to the government in 1997 recommends the elimination of this deduction, with some relief for gains accruing to the date of elimination — possibly through an election similar to that made available when the $100,000 capital gains deduction was eliminated. The government will be reviewing the recommendations of the study. That means the deduction continues to be available in the interim.

For eligibility as a QSBC, a company must be a Canadian-controlled private corporation. At least 90% of its assets must be used in an active business in Canada, and there are additional conditions that must be met for up to two years prior to the sale. Further complications will arise where there are investments in other companies.

Each individual is entitled to a cumulative capital gains deduction of $500,000. As a result, the $500,000 capital gain deduction available on the disposition of QSBC shares will be reduced by the amount of the capital gains deductions previously claimed on any property.

EXAMPLE

Capital gains deduction at work

Let's assume you elected on your 1994 tax return to have a deemed disposition **(see article 92)** of shares of public companies, and you claimed a capital gains deduction of $100,000. In 1998, you realize a $500,000 capital gain on the sale of shares of a qualified small business corporation. You are only entitled to a $400,000 capital gains deduction in 1998 because you used $100,000 of your $500,000 lifetime capital gains deduction in 1994. However, if you had previously only claimed a $60,000 capital gains deduction, you would be entitled to a $440,000 capital gains deduction in 1998.

The amount of capital gain that is eligible for the capital gains deduction may be affected by the balance in your cumulative net investment loss account (CNIL) **(see article 103)**.

▶TAX TIP
In order to qualify as a QSBC at the time of sale, it may be necessary to take steps now to remove non-qualifying assets from the company.

Although the $500,000 deduction continues to be available, it may be appropriate to consider various tax-planning techniques that can be used to obtain the deduction. Professional tax advice on these matters is the wise course to take.

94. QUALIFIED FARM PROPERTY CAPITAL GAINS DEDUCTION

"Qualified farm property" is also eligible for a $500,000 capital gains deduction. Continued availability of this deduction was also addressed in the study referred to in article 89, and a similar recommendation was made. The $500,000 capital gains deduction available on the disposition of qualified farm property will be reduced by the amount of capital gains deductions claimed on other property. In addition, the amount of gain eligible for this deduction may be affected by the balance in your cumulative net investment loss account (CNIL) **(see article 103).**

What qualifies?

In general, if you acquired certain property before June 18, 1987, and it was used in the business of farming by you or a member of your family, it will be qualified farm property. That is provided the property was use for farming in the year you sell it or in any five previous years during which you or a member of your family owned it.

If you acquired the property after June 17, 1987, you normally must own it for at least two years, been engaged in farming on a regular and continuous basis, and earned more gross income from farming than from other sources. Similar rules also apply to allow the deduction to be claimed for gains realized on the sale of shares of a family farm corporation and on an interest in a family farm partnership.

But if you made a capital gains election **(see article 92)** on property that would otherwise be considered "qualified farm property," the qualifying tests may be different than outlined above. Discuss this with your tax adviser.

> ▶ *TAX TIP*
> Professional advice from your tax adviser is recommended to determine if you are eligible for the $500,000 deduction on your farm property (or property that was formerly used in farming).

95. CAPITAL GAINS RESERVES MAY BE RESTRICTED

When you sell your real estate or another investment and the proceeds from the sale will not be all receivable in the year of sale, you can defer a portion of the capital gain by claiming a reserve.

For dispositions prior to November 13, 1981, the amount of the reserve is only subject to the limitation that it be a "reasonable" amount of the gain. A reasonable amount is generally calculated as the portion of the original gain that is still represented by uncollected proceeds — in other words, the amount that you are still owed.

However, for instalment sales made after November 12, 1981, the rules provide that at least one-fifth of your taxable capital gain must be reported in the year of sale and each of the four following years. An exception is provided if you transfer certain farm property or shares in a small business corporation to your children. In these cases, you can claim a reserve over a maximum 10-year period. Reserves deducted from income in one year must be added to income in the subsequent year.

▶ TAX TIP

Claiming a reserve is optional – any amount up to the maximum allowed can be claimed. To make a claim, you must file form T2017 with your income tax return.

Special rules

Capital gains reserves included in income will be eligible for the capital gains deduction if the property was disposed of after 1984 and is a share of a qualified small business corporation or a qualified farm property **(see articles 93 and 94)**. Special rules are provided to ensure that reserves are adjusted for changes in the capital gains inclusion rate.

Should you decide to report all of the capital gain and claim the off-setting capital gains deduction, even though a reserve is available, take care to ensure you are not caught by the alternative minimum tax **(see article 110)** or the CNIL rules **(see article 103)**.

▶ TAX TIP

In structuring the sale of property, make sure that you will have sufficient funds to pay the taxes required. If proceeds are deferred over a long period of time, the tax may be due before the proceeds are received. Suppose you sell real estate for a significant capital gain in 1998 and the proceeds are due over the next six years. The taxes arising on the capital gain must be paid in full by 2002 even though some of the proceeds are not due until 2003.

96. CAPITAL LOSS RULES

Generally, capital losses are only deductible against capital gains. But there are cases where unused allowable capital losses realized prior to May 23, 1985, can be claimed against other sources of income, at the rate of $2,000 per year. After that date, capital losses can only be claimed against capital gains. Capital losses can be carried back three years and forward indefinitely.

Restrictions on claims

With the introduction of the capital gains deduction in 1985, rules were introduced to ensure that you would not be able to claim the deduction and be able to deduct capital losses from other sources at the same time. If you claimed pre-May 23, 1985, losses against other sources of income and realize a capital gain on the disposition of shares of a qualified small business corporation or a qualified farm property, the amount of the gain eligible for the capital gains deduction could be affected.

Rules are also in effect to adjust prior years' capital loss carry-forwards for changes in the capital gains inclusion rate.

Unused capital losses from prior years may be claimed in the year of death or the immediately preceding year, first to reduce capital gains in those years. Any remaining capital losses may then be deducted from other sources of income, subject to a restriction based on the total capital gains deduction that has been claimed over the years. As these special rules on the deductibility of capital losses for deceased persons are quite complex, your tax adviser should be consulted for further details.

▶ *TAX TIP*

If you realized a capital gain in the current year, consider selling investments with accrued losses before the end of the year. Note that there are rules that will deny the loss if you sell the property to certain related parties, to your RRSP, or if you reacquire the property within 30 days. Good tax advice will steer you through this strategy.

97. BUSINESS INVESTMENT LOSSES

By realizing a capital loss on the disposition of shares or debt of a small business corporation, you may be eligible to treat the loss as a business investment loss. Three-quarters of this loss can be applied against your income from other sources, not just capital gains.

Meeting the conditions

Specific conditions must be met before a capital loss can be classified as a business investment loss. First of all, the shares or debt must be those of a small business corporation. Consult your tax adviser to determine if the corporation qualifies. In addition, if the loss results from an actual sale, you must have sold the shares or debt to a taxpayer not related to you. If the debt is established as a bad debt, you may recognize the loss even though a sale has not taken place (whether or not you are related to the corporation).

Similarly, if shares of a small business corporation are worthless, any capital loss incurred may qualify as a business investment loss. Your loss will be recognized, if you so elect, by filing a statement with your tax return, and if the following conditions apply. At the end of the year in which the loss is claimed, the company has to be insolvent and not carrying on any business (together with any company it controls). Also, the fair value of the share must be nil and it must be reasonable to assume that the company will not commence carrying on a business and will be dissolved or wound up.

If you claim the loss and the company (or another company that it controls) begins to carry on a business within two years from the end of the year in which the loss was claimed, you will have to report a corresponding capital gain in the year the business commences.

Restrictions on ABILs

Following the introduction of the lifetime capital gains deduction, rules were introduced to prevent you from claiming the deduction as well as benefiting from an allowable business investment loss (ABIL). The rules are similar to the restrictions placed on deductions for capital losses of prior years **(see article 96)**. As a result, you will not be able to claim the capital gains deduction to the extent of ABILs claimed in 1985 or later.

It's a similar situation if you have claimed the capital gains deduction (on a disposition or as a result of the capital gains election), and you realize what would otherwise be an ABIL in a subsequent year. The loss will be treated as a regular allowable capital loss, to the extent of your previously claimed capital gains deduction.

▶ *TAX TIP*
If you have loaned money to a corporation and the debt is not collectible, consider whether you have incurred an ABIL. It is important that you determine the time at which the amount becomes uncollectible. It's a definite plus to have a tax adviser in your corner if this situation arises.

98. TAXATION OF DIVIDENDS
When you receive a dividend from a Canadian corporation, the amount you report on your return is not the amount you received — it's more. Not to worry, as this actually works to your advantage.

How is dividend tax calculated?
The amount you include in your income, often referred to as the "grossed-up amount," is increased by an amount that is supposed to represent your proportion of the income taxes paid by the corporation. You are then able to claim a credit against your federal income taxes, which also reduces your provincial income taxes. The grossed-up amount is 125% of the actual dividend and the amount of the federal portion of the dividend tax credit is 16 2/3% of the actual dividend.

As a result of this gross-up and tax credit mechanism, the effective rate of tax you pay on dividends is less than the rate you pay on your other sources of income. Depending on your province of residence, the top rate on Canadian dividend income is approximately 30% to 39% as opposed to roughly 44% to 54% on other sources of income (excluding capital gains) **(see Table 4)**.

EXAMPLE
Dividend tax credit
If you received $1,000 of dividends from BCE Inc. in 1998, you must include $1,250 in your income. That makes you eligible to claim a federal tax credit of $167. If you are in the highest federal tax bracket and

your provincial tax rate is 50%, you will pay an effective tax rate of 31% on the dividend income (ignoring provincial surtaxes).

Federal tax ($1,250 x 29%)	$363
Less: Federal tax credit	(167)
	196
Federal surtax @8%	16
Provincial tax (50% x $196)	98
	$310

In the calculation above, you will pay tax at an effective rate of 31% on the $1,000 dividend received. If you had received $1,000 of interest income (from bonds or GICs), you will pay tax at an effective rate of 45.8% (ignoring provincial surtaxes).

Federal tax ($1,000 x 29%)	$290
Federal surtax @8%	23
Provincial tax (50% x $290)	145
	$458

▶ *TAX TIP*

If you have no other sources of income, you can receive approximately $23,000 in Canadian dividend income without paying any tax. The amount will vary depending on your province of residence at the end of the year.

99. TRANSFER OF DIVIDEND INCOME BETWEEN SPOUSES

If your spouse has little or no income, except for taxable dividends from Canadian corporations, you may reduce your family tax bill by including your spouse's dividends in your income.

This can only be accomplished if, by doing so, you are able to increase the claim you make for your spouse as a dependant. In effect, you delete the dividends from your spouse's income and include them in your income, entitling you to claim the dividend tax credit. The election must apply to all of your spouse's dividends from taxable Canadian corporations. You cannot pick and choose to maximize tax savings.

100. TAXATION OF INTEREST INCOME

A different set of rules is in place to determine when you must report interest income for tax purposes. Much of it depends on when the investment was purchased.

With investments made prior to 1990, you have the option of reporting interest either on an annual accrual basis or reporting the accrued interest every three years. As of January 1, 1990, individuals are required to report interest on investments made in 1990 and subsequent years on an annual basis, regardless of when the interest is actually paid. Similar rules apply to certain life insurance policies and annuity contracts.

You are also required to compute the interest on debt where the return on the investment is adjusted for inflation and/or deflation. If you own such a security, you will have to report an amount annually as interest income.

▶ *TAX TIP*

Do you own investments that earn significant interest income? There may be valid reasons for you to consider transferring them to a holding company — income splitting and estate planning, just to mention a couple. Also, depending on your provincial tax rates, a slight tax deferral may be realized where funds remain invested in the company for a period of time. Proper planning is needed to ensure that the effects of the income attribution rules are minimized. Your tax adviser can assist you with this and can best assess if it's worth your while to do so.

101. CANADA SAVINGS BONDS

Reporting income earned on Canada Savings Bonds (CSBs) can be complicated because of the two different types of bonds available — regular or compound interest. Then, just for good measure, toss in the optional reporting requirements regarding when the interest must be included in income **(see article 100)**, and you have the basis of an often confusing process. To simplify it, just remember: with regular bonds, you will receive and report the interest each year.

Compound bonds

Compound bonds are another thing entirely. If you own compound bonds, you will not receive the interest until the bond matures or is cashed in. Nevertheless, the interest must either be reported annually or every three years. The three-year accrual is only available up to Series 44 (issued in 1989), so shortly, everyone will be reporting interest annually. For compound bonds issued in 1990 and subsequent years, annual accrual is the only option available. The government will issue an information slip indicating the amount of income to be reported.

If you are using the annual or three-year accrual method, it is important to keep track of the amounts you have reported each year for each series. When the bond matures and you actually receive the interest, or if you cash your compound bond early, you will report the total interest received, less the portion of interest previously reported.

Compounding bonds Series 43 (issued in 1988) mature in November 1998. If you discover that you have not been reporting the interest on compound bonds by one of the methods noted above (annual or three-year accrual), Revenue Canada expects you to file amending information for the appropriate year.

▶ *TAX TIP*
When you purchase Canada Savings Bonds with a loan that is repaid through a payroll deduction plan, any interest you pay on the loan is deductible.

102. MUTUAL FUNDS

Mutual funds are pools of assets that are invested by professional managers, either in general investments or in a particular individual sector.

Some mutual funds pay dividends, but may designate all or a portion of the dividends as capital gains dividends to reflect capital gains earned by the mutual fund. Such dividends are treated as capital gains and are subject to the usual capital gains treatment for income tax purposes.

Special rules apply if a capital gains election was made on a mutual fund (see article 92). The capital gain elected does not increase the cost base of the mutual fund. Instead, a special tax account is created, called an "exempt capital gains balance." The balance in this account can be used to offset future capital gains designated by the fund, as well as any gain on actual disposition of the mutual fund units. In general, this account may be used within a 10-year period, and any balance remaining at the end of the year 2004 will be added to the cost base of the fund.

EXAMPLE

Capital gains in action

Let's say you made a $10,000 capital gains election in 1994 in respect of your mutual fund. In the following years the fund designates capital gains paid to you as follows:

1995	$2,500
1996	3,000
1997	3,000
	$8,500

You could use the $10,000 exempt capital gains balance created in 1994 to offset the allocated gains and you would still have an exempt capital gains balance of $1,500 remaining at the end of 1997 to shelter future gains from this mutual fund. For example, if you sold the mutual fund units in 1998 for a capital gain of $2,000, you could use your remaining balance to offset $1,500 of the gain.

▶ *TAX TIP*

The amount of exempt capital gains balance claimed in a particular year is optional — up to the amount of the capital gains designated to you by the fund or the gain on disposition. In some cases, it may pay to claim other available deductions and credits.

Under recent changes, retroactive to 1994, any unused balance in the exempt capital gains balance account at the time that all interests or shares in a particular mutual fund are disposed of may be added to the adjusted cost base of those interests or shares. This applies to dispositions of mutual funds prior to 2005. This will give recognition to the appropriate capital loss on the disposition of the mutual fund units or shares.

▶ *TAX TIP*

If you made a capital gains election on a mutual fund that you have since disposed of, you should review your tax return to determine if there was any remaining exempt capital gains balance. If a balance was remaining, you should request an adjustment to the capital gain or capital loss reported. This applies to 1994 and subsequent years. Discuss the potential adjustment and tax savings with your tax adviser.

103. CUMULATIVE NET INVESTMENT LOSS RULES

The government introduced the cumulative net investment loss (CNIL) account in 1988. It was developed to prevent individuals from reducing their income by claiming investment losses, such as rental losses and carrying charges, and subsequently recouping the losses by selling the underlying investment, and then not paying any tax on the resulting gain due to the capital gains deduction.

Due to the elimination of the $100,000 capital gains deduction on other property, your CNIL will only be relevant for years after 1994 if you have a gain from the disposition of qualified farm property or a share of a qualified small business corporation.

What is a CNIL?

Your CNIL account is the cumulative excess of your investment expenses over your investment income. Investment expenses include losses from rental property, non-active partnership losses such as tax shelters, interest on money borrowed for investments, and 50% of resource-related deductions.

Investment income includes all income from property (including rental income, interest income and dividends), non-active partnership income and 50% of natural resource income. Investment income does not include taxable capital gains, although capital gains that cannot be sheltered by the capital gains deduction reduce the impact of the CNIL account.

Since the CNIL account is a cumulative account (for 1988 and subsequent years), it is recommended that you keep a running total each year even if you are not claiming a capital gains deduction in the year. In general, you will only be able to claim the capital gains deduction to the extent your taxable capital gain for the given year exceeds the amount of your CNIL.

▶ *TAX TIP*

If you are an owner-manager of a corporation and have a CNIL problem, you should consider receiving sufficient interest or dividend income from your corporation to eliminate your CNIL.

▶ *TAX TIP*

Where possible, borrow for business purposes as opposed to investment purposes. The interest expense on funds borrowed to carry on a business or profession does not enter into the calculation of your CNIL account.

104. DEDUCTIBILITY OF INTEREST EXPENSE

Interest expense is deductible for income tax purposes provided the borrowed funds were used to earn income and certain other conditions are met. Over the years, Revenue Canada has allowed interest as a deduction even though it may not be deductible from a strictly technical point of view — for instance, if a company borrows funds to pay a dividend rather than using its own funds. However, following a 1987 Supreme Court decision, considerable uncertainty developed as to whether interest would continue to be deductible under these circumstances.

When is interest deductible?

To try to resolve this problem, Revenue Canada introduced draft legislation in 1991 regarding the deductibility of interest expense. These proposed changes deal with the deductibility of interest where borrowed money is used by corporations and partnerships to distribute retained earnings or capital.

Also included are provisions relating to borrowings made by shareholders and partners in order to loan money to a corporation or partnership, or to honour a guarantee of its indebtedness. Borrowings used to acquire shares, and to make interest-free or low-interest loans to shareholders or employees, are also covered.

A fixed date has still not been set for the implementation of any of these changes. Revenue Canada has noted that it intends to follow current assessing practices until the final legislation is formally introduced. In general, interest will be deductible if the funds were borrowed to pay dividends or redeem shares, provided the amount of the dividend or redemption does not exceed the accumulated profits of the company.

Funds borrowed by individual shareholders to loan to their corporation at no interest or low interest will continue to be deductible. But as usual, there is a catch. The funds must be used by the company to earn income, no unfair advantage can be derived, and the company cannot obtain the same terms of financing from a third party without the guarantee of the individual.

Check before borrowing
As final legislation could be introduced at any time and current assessing practices are subject to change, you should check with your tax adviser to determine Revenue Canada's position if you are borrowing funds for any of these purposes.

During the 1980s, a series of cases stressed the link between a source of income and the related interest expense. The courts established that, where a source of income disappeared, the deductibility of interest on money borrowed to acquire the source ceased.

For example, if money was borrowed to acquire shares and the shares were subsequently sold at a loss, or were lost due to the bankruptcy of the company, the interest ceased to be deductible. Legislation was introduced, effective for 1994 and later years, that may permit a continued deduction for interest expense. Due to the complexity of the rules, professional tax advice is recommended.

▶ *TAX TIP*
When you borrow, try to borrow for investment or business purposes before you borrow for personal reasons. Conversely, when repaying debt consider repaying loans on which interest is non-deductible before you repay those on which the interest is deductible. After all, why would you prematurely eliminate an arrangement that provides a measure of tax relief?

In one recent court case dealing with interest deductibility, the taxpayers borrowed funds to acquire common shares in offshore corporations. The taxpayers disposed of their shares after several years and reported substantial capital gains.

Although the deductibility of interest with respect to funds used to acquire common shares is generally not an issue, the taxpayers were not allowed to deduct their interest expense. The government took the position that the borrowed funds had not been used to earn income from a business or property, and that the taxpayers had no reasonable expectation of profit from the dividend payments. The real purpose of the investment was to realize a capital gain on their investment.

Although this case is currently under appeal, it restates Revenue Canada's position that interest on funds borrowed to realize capital gains is not deductible. If you borrow to invest in certain types of mutual funds, you should be aware of this position.

105. RESOURCE SECTOR AS A TAX SHELTER

Most investors do not invest directly in the resource sector. Rather, they obtain tax writeoffs by investing in limited partnerships created for that purpose, or by investing in shares of companies (flow-through shares), whereby the companies pass on the deductions to the shareholders, who claim them on their own tax returns.

Junior oil and gas sector

To stimulate investment in the junior oil and gas sector, the first $1 million of eligible Canadian Development Expenses (CDE) that are renounced by a company under a flow-through share agreement can be reclassified as Canadian Exploration Expenses (CEE). This allows shareholders to deduct 100% of such expenses (rather than the 30% rate that is currently allowed for CDE). Changes made in 1996 reduced the reclassification limit from the previous limit of $2 million and restricted its availability to corporations with less than $15 million of taxable capital employed in Canada.

106. LIMITED PARTNERSHIPS

Another type of tax shelter involves the purchase of an interest in a limited partnership. In this type of arrangement, you share the profits or loss of the business with the other partners and report a percentage of the partnership's income or loss directly as your income or loss. However, your liability with respect to the partnership's debts is limited. In general, you can lose only up to your original investment.

Restrictions

Although a limited partnership may be an attractive investment if the partnership business is expected to have losses in its initial years but is anticipated to eventually show a profit, special rules prevent you from writing off more than the amount you have invested in the partnership.

The writeoff you may claim is further restricted if the purchase of an interest is financed with certain types of "limited recourse" financing. Recent changes will also require certain partnerships to prorate expenditures, which would otherwise be deductible in the current year, over a longer term. These, along with other changes, have substantially reduced the attractiveness of limited partnerships as a tax shelter.

As you would with any other investment, you should thoroughly evaluate the investment potential of a tax shelter. It does not make any economic sense to invest in a shelter if there is little chance of either earning a return on your investment or recovering the amount you have at risk.

The alternative minimum tax (AMT) **(see article 110)** and CNIL rules **(see article 103)**, as well as restrictions on the deductibility of limited partnership losses, make it imperative that you pursue expert tax advice about your situation before making an investment.

107. TAXATION OF TRUSTS

A trust is an arrangement under which a trustee holds property for the benefit of one or more beneficiaries. It can be created at any time, including on death through one's will. Trusts are taxed as separate taxpayers. A trust created on death is taxed at the same rate as an individual, while other trusts are taxed at the highest marginal individual rate of tax (approximately 50%, depending on the province in which the trust is taxed).

Flexibility in taxation
The income of the trust will be subject to tax, but there is flexibility in the determination of exactly who gets taxed. If the trust agreement requires that the income be paid to beneficiaries, the general rule is that the beneficiaries will pay the tax. However, it is possible to make an election to have some or all of the income taxed in the trust. Alternatively, the trust agreement may provide that the income be retained in the trust for a set period of time. In this case, the general rule is that the trust will pay the tax.

> **TAX TIP**
> Consider revising your will to create separate testamentary trusts for each of your beneficiaries. This will help them save income tax on income they will earn on money you plan to leave them in your will.

The preferred beneficiary election allows the trustee and the beneficiary to retain the income in the trust while having that income taxed in the hands of the beneficiary. This election is available if the beneficiary is entitled to claim a tax credit because of a mental or physical impairment. It applies only to the beneficiary's share of the trust income. As well, this election has been extended to adult beneficiaries who are dependent on others by virtue of the beneficiaries' mental or physical infirmity.

> **TAX TIP**
> Consider creating a trust to hold investments for the benefit of a child or parent with a physical or mental disability. The income can be retained in the trust and the income may be taxed at a lower rate. This can effectively reduce taxes while allowing the trustee to control the investments.

The 21-year rule

Along with the introduction in 1972 of the tax on capital gains came the 21-year rule that prevents the indefinite deferral of tax on accrued gains on property held in trusts. Under this rule, every 21 years the trust is deemed to dispose of all its property for proceeds equal to the fair market value of the property.

Just before the first disposition of property under the 21-year rule would have arisen in 1993, the government responded to pressure to provide relief from this provision. A trustee was permitted to elect, in certain circumstances, to defer the application of the 21-year rule.

The government subsequently took a second look at this matter and decided that either the 21-year rule would be applied to tax accrued gains in 1993 or that the gains would be deemed to have been realized on January 1, 1999. If the trustee revoked the earlier election before 1997, the gains would be taxed in 1993. If not revoked, the deemed disposition will generally arise on January 1, 1999.

▶ *TAX TIP*
It may be possible, if the trust agreement so permits, to avoid this deemed disposition of property on January 1, 1999, by distributing the property with the accrued gain to the beneficiaries before that date. Trustees should contact their tax advisers to determine the course of action to follow.

108. FOREIGN TAXES ON INVESTMENT INCOME

As a resident of Canada, you are subject to Canadian income taxes on all your income, even if it was earned in another country. Along with interest or dividend income received from a foreign source, you must also declare as income the total of foreign taxes withheld. The foreign income is to be converted into Canadian dollars by using the average rate of exchange for 1998 or the actual exchange rate in effect when you received the income.

Foreign tax credits
You can claim a foreign tax credit for taxes withheld by the foreign country. In most cases, if the amount of foreign taxes withheld exceeds 15% of such income, the excess cannot be claimed as a foreign tax credit. You may be able to deduct the excess tax paid as an expense against that foreign income. The foreign tax credit is calculated on a per-country basis and separate calculations are required for business income tax and non-business income tax.

▶ *TAX TIP*
Revenue Canada recently released two documents that outline their assessing position on the foreign tax credits that can be claimed by U.S. citizens who are resident in Canada. The impact of the assessing position could be substantial. U.S. citizens resident in Canada should therefore review with their tax adviser the possible effects of this assessing position.

109. NEW FOREIGN REPORTING REQUIREMENTS

Many offshore investment vehicles rely on the fact that the taxpayer's interest in the offshore entity is unknown to the Canadian authorities. The government is aware of this shortcoming and is taking steps to get into the know. The first step is to induce taxpayers to comply with the Canadian tax system, and to that end, new foreign reporting requirements have been introduced.

Generally, these requirements are effective for taxation years commencing after 1995. However, the filing deadline for information returns relating to the 1996 taxation year — and in some cases the 1997 and 1998 taxation years — were extended.

What to report

Reporting may be required if a taxpayer has transferred or loaned funds or property to a foreign-based trust, received funds or property from or is indebted to a foreign-based trust, or has a foreign affiliate. Substantial penalties may be imposed for failure to disclose the required information.

Loans and transfers to foreign trusts

If a taxpayer has transferred or loaned funds or property to a foreign-based trust at any time before the end of the trust's tax year, form T1141 must be filed by the due date for the taxpayer's return for the particular year that includes the end of the trust's year before which a transfer was made, or during which the non-resident trust was indebted to the taxpayer.

Returns must be completed for trust tax years that begin after 1995. For a trust year ending in 1996, 1997 or 1998, form T1141 is required to be filed on or before April 30, 1998, or the day on which the return is otherwise required to be filed as noted above, whichever is the later.

For example, a corporation with a March 31 year-end transfers property to a foreign-based trust on June 30, 1998. The year-end of the trust is July 31. Since the March 31, 1999, year-end of the corporation includes the July 31, 1998, year-end of the trust — the year-end of the trust during which the transfer was made — form T1141 must be filed by September 30, 1999, which is the filing due date for the corporation's 1999 tax return.

Distributions by and loans from foreign trusts

If a taxpayer has received funds or property from or is indebted to a foreign-based trust, form T1142 must be filed by the due date of the taxpayer's tax return for the particular year during which a distribution was received, or during which the taxpayer was indebted to the foreign-based trust. In the case of a partnership, the form must be filed by the due date for the partnership information return, whether or not such a return is required to be filed.

Returns must be completed for tax years that begin after 1995. For a tax year ending in 1996, 1997 or 1998, form T1142 is required to be filed on or before the later of April 30, 1998, or the day on which or before which the return is otherwise required to be filed, as noted above.

For example, an individual receives a distribution of funds from a trust on October 31, 1998. Form T1142 must be filed by the due date of the individual's 1998 tax return either — April 30, 1999, or June 15, 1999.

Interest in foreign affiliates

Taxpayers who own shares of foreign affiliates are also required to file an information return annually. The information return — form T1134-A or T1134-B, as appropriate — must be filed no later than 15 months after the end of the taxation year for which it is filed.

However, for taxation years ending in 1996, 1997 and 1998, the filing due date is June 30, 1998, or 15 months after the end of the taxation year, whichever is the later. For example, a corporation with a December 31, 1997, year-end is required to file this information return no later than March 31, 1999.

Foreign property holdings

The new reporting obligations requiring taxpayers with interests in certain foreign property (shares, bank accounts, real property, etc.) in excess of $100,000 to report and provide details on such holdings have been deferred. Revenue Canada announced the first filing deadline for these returns will not be before April 30, 1999.

Returns will not be required for the 1996 or 1997 taxation years. As a result of public outcry, the Auditor General of Canada examined this particular reporting requirement to assess whether it is the appropriate approach to ensure the proper reporting of world income. The Auditor General reached the conclusion that the requirement is appropriate and justified. Taxpayers should be prepared to file the required information return for 1998. Certain foreign property, such as personal-use property and property that is used in carrying on an active business, is excluded from this reporting requirement.

▶ **TAX TIP**
Does your portfolio include foreign investments? Then it's time to consult with your tax adviser to review filing requirements. In some cases, the information you are required to report will not be readily available and time will be needed to accumulate it. Failure to comply with these requirements can result in penalties.

110. ALTERNATIVE MINIMUM TAX

The purpose of the alternative minimum tax (AMT) is to restrict the tax benefits derived from various tax preference items such as approved tax shelters, pension deductions, capital gains, investment tax credits and other items. It either imposes an overall limit on the total of these identified deductions, credits and exclusions, or reduces the tax savings derived from these items.

You should not have to pay AMT unless your tax preference items exceed a $40,000 exemption. Even then, depending on your circumstances, the total of such items may significantly exceed this limit before AMT is triggered. In many cases, AMT will not be due. Additionally, it does not apply in the year of death.

EXAMPLE

The AMT calculation

AMT is calculated as 17% of the amount by which your "adjusted taxable income" exceeds the exemption of $40,000. Your adjusted taxable income is your taxable income determined for ordinary tax purposes adjusted to add back certain deductions ("tax preference items"), which are not allowed as deductions for determining AMT.

If your AMT exceeds the amount of your regular federal taxes payable, the AMT becomes the amount of federal tax used to determine your tax liability. From this amount you subtract the tax credits (i.e., personal tax credit, spousal amount, etc.) that are allowable for AMT purposes and make all other necessary tax calculations (i.e., surtaxes, other credits and provincial taxes).

Relief in future years

If you have to pay AMT, you will pay more tax than that required under the regular rules. Don't worry, though, as you are entitled to a credit for the excess in future years when your regular tax liability exceeds your AMT for that year. The carry-forward period is seven years, and the credit each year cannot reduce your liability below your AMT amount for that year.

As noted above, one of the restricted tax benefits is pension deductions. The 1998 federal budget proposes for 1998 and subsequent years that contributions to an RRSP or RPP will not have an impact on AMT, even if the contribution is larger than normal, such as could be the case if you received a retiring allowance.

If you were subject to AMT in any year from 1994 to 1997 because of a RRSP or RPP deduction, it is proposed that the portion of the AMT you paid, because of the RRSP or RPP deduction, be refunded to you. That is unless you have already recovered the AMT in a previous year as explained above. If you paid AMT in one of those years, you should consult with your tax adviser to ensure that you get the correct refund.

In This Section

Employees

Much of what a working taxpayer needs to know about his or her tax situation can be found in Section 2, which deals with individual taxpayers. However, if you are an employee of a company, you could also be in line for some added tax advantages and, at the same time, be liable for several other tax obligations. The following 15 items take a look at those specific situations and how they could apply to you.

If you have use of a company-owned vehicle, or your employer has provided a low-interest or interest-free loan, this section gives you the lowdown on what to expect, and how to ensure that taxes are kept to a minimum. The following items also tell you what is involved when you take a temporary assignment outside of Canada, and how you can utilize the overseas investment tax credit.

If the company you work for provides you with the opportunity to acquire stock options, there are rules you need to know about. Rules that cover commissioned salespersons, home office expenses, legal expenses and death benefits are also included, along with detailed information regarding company and individual pension plans.

111. TAX-FREE TRAVEL ALLOWANCES

If you use your own car for work, you may be eligible to receive a tax-free allowance from your employer to cover your travel expenses. The allowance qualifies for tax-free status if it is reasonable and only if it is based on the actual number of kilometres that the car is used for business purposes.

Allowances that are not based upon the number of kilometres driven, such as a flat allowance of $400 per month, must be included in income. Your employer can reimburse you for certain limited expenses — supplementary business insurance, parking costs incurred for business purposes, toll and ferry charges — without affecting the tax-free status of the allowance, provided the per-kilometre requirement is met.

▶ **TAX TIP**
If the business portion of your travel expenses exceeds the amount of your tax-free allowance, consider including the allowance in income and claiming related expenses. To do this, the allowance must be considered unreasonable. Since this treatment has been the subject of some recent court cases, professional advice may be required.

EXAMPLE

Travel expense options

Let's assume, in the course of your work, you incurred business travel expenses of $1,000, for which you received a tax-free allowance of $800 from your employer in 1998. You could simply prepare your tax return without reporting the allowance or claiming any of the deductions. Alternatively, include the allowance in your income and claim the deduction, resulting in a net deduction of $200.

GST rebate

You may be able to claim a GST rebate for expenses that are deductible in computing your income for tax purposes. However, this rebate is generally only available if you do not receive a per-kilometre allowance from your employer. In addition, you must be employed by a GST registrant other than a listed financial institution such as a bank, insurance company or brokerage firm.

This rebate is calculated as 7/107ths of eligible expenses if you live outside the harmonized tax provinces of Newfoundland and Labrador, New Brunswick and Nova Scotia. In those provinces, the rebate is generally 15/115ths of the eligible expenses. Although the rebate claim must be filed with your income tax return, you still have up to four years to file a claim.

GST and allowances

The rules are more complicated if you received an allowance from your employer to cover expenses. Your employer must certify on a prescribed form that the allowance was not considered to be "reasonable" at the time it was paid. An allowance may not be reasonable in amount or it may be deemed to be unreasonable because it is not calculated solely on kilometres driven.

For instance, a flat allowance of $400 a month is not "reasonable" while an allowance of $2 a kilometre is likely unreasonably high. If your employer signs the required form, you can claim a GST rebate equal to 7/107 (or 15/115 in the participating provinces) of your net eligible expenses. In this situation, your employer is not entitled to claim an input tax credit for the allowance.

▶ **TAX TIP**
Where an employee receives an allowance that is not sufficient to cover the business portion of expenses, the employee may take the position that the allowance is unreasonably low, take the allowance into income, and deduct the actual expenses incurred. The employer and employee should review the GST treatment of the allowance.

If the employer agrees that the allowance is unreasonably low and certifies this on the prescribed form, the employee can claim a GST rebate. But, if the employer believes the allowance is reasonable, the employee cannot claim a rebate, and an employer can claim an input tax credit for GST on the allowance. Review your employment arrangement to see if any changes should be made to accommodate these rules.

▶ **TAX TIP**
Did you fail to claim the GST rebate in prior years? Then get busy – you can still file a claim for 1995, 1996 and 1997 at the same time you file your 1998 personal tax return.

112. PERSONAL USE OF A COMPANY-OWNED AUTOMOBILE

Part of your employment package may have your employer providing you with an automobile. If so, you will have to report a taxable benefit based upon a "standby charge," which reflects your access to the car, and an operating benefit, which reflects the personal portion of operating expenses paid by your employer.

In general, the standby charge is 2% of the original cost of the car, including GST and PST, for each month in the year the car is made available for your use. If the car is leased, the standby charge is two-thirds of the lease cost, net of insurance costs.

▶ *TAX TIP*

You may be able to reduce the standby charge if you use the vehicle 90% or more for business purposes. Maintaining accurate mileage records to support this claim should be made part of your daily routine.

▶ *TAX TIP*

The standby charge is calculated on the original cost of the car and does not decrease as the car's value declines with age. After a few years, it may be cheaper to eliminate this benefit by buying the car from your employer.

Provided certain conditions are met, individuals employed in selling or leasing automobiles may qualify for a reduced standby charge. In these cases, the standby charge generally is computed at 1.5% instead of 2%.

Operating cost

Generally, the "operating cost" benefit is calculated as 14 cents per kilometre for personal use, less amounts paid by you to your employer in respect of the operating costs. This amount includes a GST component.

If the automobile is used primarily (more than 50%) for employment purposes, there is an optional formula that can be used to determine the operating cost benefit. It can be calculated as 50% of the standby charge.

▶ *TAX TIP*

Keep records detailing the personal and business use of the car to determine which option is more beneficial. If you want the optional formula to apply for a given year, you must notify your employer in writing before the end of the year. It is important to keep accurate mileage records as the onus will be on you to prove the amount of business use. Review the automobile arrangement to ensure that the real benefit, if any, justifies the complex record keeping required. Alternative arrangements of monthly allowances or mileage compensation may provide better real compensation and ease the paper burden.

113. LOW-INTEREST OR INTEREST-FREE LOANS TO EMPLOYEES

Employers occasionally provide employees with low-interest or interest-free loans. If you have received such a loan, you may have to report a taxable benefit based on a prescribed rate of interest that is adjusted quarterly. These rules also apply to shareholder loans that are not required to be included in income **(see article 7)**.

▶ *TAX TIP*

If you received a low-interest loan from your employer, make sure you pay the yearly interest on the loan by January 30 of the following year. If you pay the prior year's interest after January 30, the payment will not reduce the taxable benefit for the preceding year, nor will it reduce the taxable benefit for the current year.

Using the loan to acquire investments or to earn income, as opposed to using the funds for personal purposes, allows you to claim the amount of the taxable benefit as a deductible interest expense.

▶ *TAX TIP*

Did you receive a low-interest or interest-free loan from your employer? And did you use the proceeds for investment purposes? Then make sure you claim the deemed interest deduction.

Home relocation loans

You've been asked to begin work at a new location and your employer has kindly extended to you a low-interest or interest-free loan to help you buy a home. The taxable benefit arising from this arrangement may be partially or entirely offset by a special deduction.

To qualify, your new residence must be at least 40 kilometres closer to your new work location than your old residence. In general, this special deduction will entirely offset the taxable benefit arising from low-interest or interest-free loans of $25,000 or less. This deduction applies for a five-year period commencing on the date you received the loan.

Under certain circumstances, some or all of the interest benefit from a home relocation loan made to an employee is not taxable. Interest benefits on such loans made after February 23, 1998, are taxable subject to the special home relocation loan deduction.

▶ TAX TIPS

If you think you qualify for this "home relocation loan" but the special deduction is not identified on your T4 slip, check with your employer.

If you received a low-interest or interest-free loan from your employer prior to February 23, 1998, as a result of a relocation to an area with higher housing costs, you may not be required to report an interest benefit in respect of the loan.

There are also special rules if you have or are about to receive a "home purchase loan." It is not necessary for you to move to a new work location to qualify under this rule. You only have to borrow the money to either purchase or refinance the debt on your home. The benefit from such loans is computed by applying either the prescribed rate at the time the loan is granted or the prescribed rate for the particular quarter, whichever is lower. A new base rate on your loan will be established every five years.

EXAMPLE

Home loan calculation

You received a $50,000 home purchase loan on January 1, 1998, when Revenue Canada's prescribed rate was 4%. The prescribed rate increased to 5% for the second and third quarters, and assume it remains there for the rest of the year. Since the prescribed rate never fell below the rate in effect at the time the loan was granted, the benefit from the loan in 1998 is calculated using 4%. The benefit for 1998 is $2,000 (4% x $50,000). If the fourth-quarter rate was actually 3%, the 1998 benefit would be $1,873 (4% x $50,000 x 273/365) + (3% x $50,000 x 92/365).

Assuming the loan qualifies as a home relocation loan, you will be entitled to claim an offsetting deduction equal to the taxable benefit calculated on the first $25,000 of this loan — in this example, 50% of the benefit.

114. THE SCORE ON STOCK OPTIONS

Employers often provide their employees with the right to acquire shares in the company at a stated price for a stated period of time. Normally, the shares will be worth more than the purchase price at the time the employee exercises the option.

For example, your employer may offer you an option to buy 1,000 shares in the company at $5 each. When the stock price rises to $10, you exercise your option to buy the shares for $5,000. Since their current value is $10,000, you have a profit of $5,000.

How is the benefit taxed?

The income tax consequences of exercising your option depend on whether your employer is a Canadian-controlled private corporation (CCPC), the period of time you hold the shares before eventually selling them, and whether you deal at arm's length with your employer.

If your employer is a CCPC, there will not be any income tax consequences until you dispose of the shares, provided you are not related to the controlling shareholders of the company. Shares acquired before May 23, 1985, will be taxed as a capital gain at the time the shares are actually sold to a third party. For shares acquired after May 22, 1985, the difference between the fair market value of the shares at the time the option was exercised and the option price will be taxed as employment income in the year the shares are sold.

You will be able to claim a deduction equal to one-quarter of this amount if certain conditions are met. Three-quarters of the difference between the ultimate sale price and the fair market value of the shares at the date the option was exercised will be a taxable capital gain. As such, it may be eligible for the $500,000 capital gains deduction for shares of a qualified small business corporation **(see article 93)**.

EXAMPLE

Cashing in on stock options

Your employer is a CCPC and in 1997 all employees were offered an option to buy 1,000 shares in the company at $1 each. In 1998, the company goes public and the stock performs very well. At the end of 1998, the stock is trading at $2 per share and you decide to exercise your option. The price jumps to $3 in early 2001 and you decide to sell all of your shares. Since your employer was a CCPC at the time the option was granted, there is no taxable benefit until you sell the shares in 2001. The benefit is calculated as follows:

Employment Income:	
Employment income ($2 - $1) x (1,000 shares)	$1,000
Income deduction (25%)	(250)
Income inclusion	$750
Capital Gain:	
Proceeds of disposition ($3 x 1,000 shares)	$3,000
Cost base ($2 x 1,000 shares)	
(2,000)	
Capital Gain	1,000
	75%
Taxable Capital Gain	$750

Different treatment for public companies

If your employer is a public company or not a CCPC, you are not so lucky. The difference between the fair market value of the shares at the time the option is exercised and the option price is taxable as employment income in the year you exercise the option. However, where the options were granted after February 15, 1984, and provided certain conditions are met, you may deduct one-quarter of this deemed benefit from your taxable income.

Options held at the date of death

If an employee owns unexercised options under an employee stock option plan, here's what happens if he or she passes away. The difference between the fair market value of options held immediately before death and the price paid to acquire the option must be reported as employment income on the taxpayer's final income tax return.

It may be possible to claim a deduction equal to one-quarter of this income inclusion. If the stock option is exercised or otherwise disposed of within the first taxation year of the estate, here's what the taxpayer's legal representative can do. He or she can elect to treat any decline in value — from the date of death to the date of exercise or sale — as a loss from employment for the year in which the taxpayer died.

115. DEDUCTIONS FROM EMPLOYMENT INCOME RESTRICTED

As an employee, your eligible deductions from employment income are limited. With certain restrictions, you may deduct registered pension plan (RPP) contributions, annual professional and union dues, automobile expenses, home office expenses, legal fees incurred to collect or establish a right to salary, as well as the cost of supplies consumed directly in the performance of your employment duties. Canada Pension Plan (CPP) contributions and employment insurance (EI) premiums are eligible for a non-refundable tax credit equal to 17% of the required contributions — this equates to a tax savings of approximately 26% after taking provincial taxes into account.

There is a host of other deductions available if you are a commissioned salesperson **(see article 119)**, or for travel expenses, if you are required to perform your duties away from your employer's place of business.

116. AUTOMOBILE EXPENSES YOU CAN CLAIM

You may be eligible to claim automobile expenses if you use your automobile for employment purposes. To claim your automobile, the vehicle must be required for you to carry on your employment or office duties away from the employer's place of business, and the automobile expenses incurred result from carrying out these duties. Further, you cannot claim auto expenses if you are in receipt of a tax-free allowance for auto usage from your employer **(see article 111)**.

Expenses that can be claimed include such items as gas, repairs and maintenance, insurance, interest paid on the automobile loan, lease payments and depreciation on the automobile. Restrictions are imposed on the amount of interest, depreciation and lease payments that may be claimed **(see article 16)**.

Calculating your claim

The actual claim is calculated by applying the total of all the expenses noted above to the percentage of use relevant for employment purposes. For example, your automobile claim may be determined by dividing the kilometres driven for employment purposes over the total kilometres driven for the year. If there were any reimbursements made by your employer for automobile expenses, the reimbursement must be deducted from the expense claim.

As is the case with most tax deductions, supporting documentation and accurate records should be maintained. Your employer must sign form T2200 outlining the conditions of employment and the form is required to be filed with the tax return.

117. HOME OFFICE EXPENSES

Does your job require you to work at home? Then you may be eligible to claim the use of a portion of your home as an office expense. You will only be permitted to deduct costs related to a home office if your work space is either the place where you principally perform your employment duties or is used exclusively on a regular and continuous basis for meeting people while performing your employment duties.

As an employee, the home office expenses that you can claim are restricted. If you own your home, your deductions are limited to the maintenance of the premises, such as a portion of fuel, electricity and minor repairs. You cannot deduct mortgage interest or any depreciation on your home. However, if you are a commission salesperson, your deductions may include property taxes and insurance. If you pay rent, a proportionate amount of the rent is deductible.

You cannot create a loss from employment by claiming home office expenses. However, any eligible expenses that you cannot use in one year can be carried forward to subsequent years. The rules are comparable to the rules for self-employed individuals **(see article 12)**.

▶ *TAX TIP*

Your employer must certify on form T2200 that you are required under your contract of employment to use a portion of your home as an office. This form must be filed with your income tax return.

118. LEGAL EXPENSES

Legal costs paid to collect or establish a right to salary or wages from your employer or former employer are deductible. In a parallel battle with an employer, legal expenses paid to collect or establish a right to a retiring allowance or pension benefit are also deductible within a seven-year carry-forward period. The deduction is limited to the amount of retiring allowance or pension benefits received less any portion that has been transferred to an RPP or RRSP.

119. DEDUCTIONS FOR COMMISSION SALESPERSONS

An employed commission salesperson required to pay expenses should be aware of the deductions that may be claimed. You may deduct all expenses, other than capital items, you incurred that are directly related to earning your commissions. For example, you may claim automobile and other travel expenses, advertising, promotion and telephone expenses. However, the total claim cannot exceed your commission income.

Expenses for meals and entertainment are limited to 50% of their actual cost **(see article 14)**. To deduct the cost of meals while travelling, you must be away from the municipality where your employer is located for at least 12 hours. You may also be able to deduct a portion of your home as an office expense **(see article 117)**.

There are numerous restrictions regarding the amounts you can deduct for automobile expenses **(see article 16)**. In order to support any claim, it is vital you maintain thorough records and relevant documentation for all expenditures. However, this supporting documentation does not have to be submitted with your personal income tax return.

> ♦ *TAX TIP*
>
> In general, you can only claim interest expense and depreciation on the business-use portion of your automobile expenses. All other assets, such as computers and other office equipment, are not depreciable, nor can you deduct the interest paid on a loan taken out to acquire such assets. For this reason, it may be preferable to lease such assets rather than purchase them.

Your employer must certify on form T2200 that you are required to incur the expenses you are claiming, and this form must be included with your tax return.

120. SPECIAL RULES FOR ARTISTS AND ENTERTAINERS

Artists and entertainers are entitled to special treatment under the Income Tax Act.

If you are employed as a musician and are required to provide a musical instrument as a condition of your employment, you may deduct the cost of maintenance, rent or capital cost allowance **(see article 10)** and insurance for the instrument. The amount deducted for musical instrument costs cannot exceed the income from employment as a musician, after you deduct all other employment expenses.

Artists and entertainers receiving employment income are entitled to deduct related expenses actually incurred up to a maximum of 20% of such income, but not more than $1,000. This deduction is in addition to the deductions that all employees may be entitled to for most other expenses, such as automobile and related travelling expenses. However, it is reduced by the sum of the amounts claimed for interest and capital cost allowance on an automobile and for musical instrument costs (see above).

> ▶ *TAX TIP*
> Expenses incurred in the year, but restricted by the 20% or $1,000 limit, may be carried forward indefinitely. Don't overlook these carry-forward balances when calculating your income from artistic employment.

121. TEMPORARY ASSIGNMENTS OUTSIDE CANADA

Many employee relocations are only temporary, ranging from a few weeks to several years. For income tax purposes, it is important that you determine your residency status during the period you are outside Canada. A resident of Canada is taxed on his or her worldwide income. Therefore, if you are a Canadian resident for income tax purposes, any employment income you earn during an assignment abroad will be subject to Canadian tax.

Residency defined

Residence is a question of fact, and surprisingly the term "resident" is not defined in the Income Tax Act. The courts, however, have held that you are a resident of Canada for tax purposes if Canada is the place you regularly or customarily live.

Revenue Canada applies a general rule of thumb — unless the circumstances indicate otherwise, you will be considered a non-resident if you are absent from Canada for two years or longer. However, if your return to Canada is foreseeable at the time of departure, you will not necessarily lose your status of Canadian residence for income tax purposes, solely because of an absence of more than two years.

Canada also has income tax treaties with a number of countries and these treaties contain tie-breaker rules to determine residency when you appear to be a resident of two countries.

▶ *TAX TIP*
Depending on the circumstances, your residency status and the time of taking up residency may be difficult to ascertain. A discussion with your tax adviser is strongly recommended well in advance of any move into or out of Canada.

If you cease to be a resident of Canada for income tax purposes, special rules apply **(see article 80)**.

122. OVERSEAS EMPLOYMENT TAX CREDIT

If you were employed by a Canadian company, or by a corporation that is a foreign affiliate of your Canadian employer, and you have performed most or all of your work outside Canada for a period of more than six consecutive months, you may be eligible for a special tax credit. To qualify, you must be a resident of Canada for income tax purposes.

The credit eliminates tax on 80% of your eligible income up to a maximum of $100,000. Maximum eligible income is reduced if your time spent on the qualifying activity in a given year was less than the entire year. Qualified activities include construction, installation, engineering, agriculture and the exploration or exploitation of oil, natural gas and minerals. Time spent negotiating contracts for these activities also qualifies.

As of 1997, new rules may limit the availability of the credit. They apply where the employer carries on a business of providing services, does not employ more than five full-time employees in the business throughout the year, and the employee owns shares in or does not deal at arm's length with the employer.

123. DEATH BENEFITS

A death benefit is an amount paid to a spouse or other beneficiary in recognition of the deceased's employment service. Up to $10,000 per deceased employee will not be taxable to the recipient(s). If there is more than one recipient, the exemption is allocated among the beneficiaries. The total deduction cannot exceed $10,000, even if the death benefit is received over a two-year period.

▶ TAX TIP

You may wish to negotiate a provision in your employment contract for the payment of a death benefit to your spouse or beneficiaries in the event of your death.

124. COMPANY PENSION PLANS

Since 1991, substantial changes have been made to all tax-deferred savings plans, including registered pension plans (RPPs).

There are two types of RPPs: defined benefit plans, in which pension benefits are specified in the plan, and money purchase plans, in which pension benefits are based on combined employer/employee contributions plus earnings in the plan.

Defined benefit plans

As a member of a defined benefit plan, you are entitled to deduct 100% of all required contributions for current or post-1989 past service. You are also entitled to deduct a maximum of $3,500 per year for past-service contributions for service prior to 1990 while you were not a contributor to a pension plan, subject to an overall limit of $3,500 times the number of years of pre-1990 service bought back. This is in addition to any deduction for current or post-1989 service.

For years of pre-1990 service during which you were a contributor to the plan, the annual deduction is limited to $3,500 less the amount of other contributions deducted in the current year. This includes amounts for the current year, post-1989 past service, as well as pre-1990 past services while you were not a contributor. The $3,500 annual limit for deductibility of pre-1990 service contributions is disregarded in the year of death. You should consult with your tax adviser if you are subject to these complicated rules.

EXAMPLE

Defined benefit contribution

Assume you make a $4,000 contribution to your defined benefit plan in 1998 in respect of two years of service prior to 1990 while you were not a contributor to a pension plan. Your maximum deduction is $3,500 in 1998. The remaining $500 can be deducted in 1999.

Money purchase plans

You are entitled to deduct the amount you contributed to a money purchase plan during the year, subject to certain maximum amounts. For example, the maximum combined employer/employee contribution for 1998 is $13,500. Money purchase plans do not allow for past-service contributions.

The benefits you earn in your defined benefit pension plan, or total contributions to a money purchase plan, determine how much you can also contribute to your RRSP **(see article 42).**

▶ *TAX TIP*

Individuals who leave registered pension plans before retirement may be able to have lost RRSP contribution room restored. The 1997 federal budget introduced a pension adjustment reversal to achieve this. The registered pension plan administrator is required to report the pension adjustment reversal to Revenue Canada. Pension adjustment reversals for terminations after 1997 will be added to the individual's RRSP contribution room for the year of termination. Pension adjustment reversals for terminations in 1997 will be added to RRSP contribution room for 1998 **(see article 42)**.

125. INDIVIDUAL PENSION PLANS

Prior to 1991, employees who held at least 10% of their company's shares were not permitted to participate in a company registered pension plan, unless the value of benefits provided to non-shareholder employees was at least equal to the value of the benefits provided to themselves. However, since 1991, employees can now become members of a single-member pension plan, regardless of their share ownership.

What is an IPP?

The individual pension plan (IPP) is simply a defined benefit pension plan for one member. Subject to certain limitations, a defined benefit plan will provide for an annual pension equal to a percentage of your highest earnings over a given period. These plans can be either 100% funded by the employer or employer/employee funded. In general, you will not be able to fund more than 50% of the cost of the pension.

IPPs are not for everyone. The decision has to be an individual one based on several factors — your age, current and projected income level, the rate of return earned on the plan's assets, whether you are an owner-manager or an arm's-length executive, as well as several other considerations. Due to their complex nature, it is recommended that you consult with your tax adviser before investing in one of these plans.

In This Section

Everyone

This final section of *Smart Tax Tips* deals with topics that are endemic to most taxpayers, whether you are a business owner, would-be entrepreneur, employee, homemaker, retiree or anyone else who has to file an income tax return, especially if there are taxes owing.

There are about a dozen items here for your consideration. There's some insight into how Revenue Canada works, what it expects you to do and what it will initiate if you can't comply. Explained concisely are collection procedures Revenue Canada undertakes, penalties and interest you can expect, and the approaches you can employ to mitigate the situation to the satisfaction of both parties.

Also presented in this section is the use of filing of your tax return electronically via EFILE, and the recent introduction TELEFILE, another filing option available to some taxpayers.

126. UNDERSTAND THE RULES BEFORE YOU ACT

Considering a financial transaction that is not part of your ordinary routine? It stands to reason that you should be up on all of the tax rules that apply to your proposed action. Taxation in Canada is for the most part quite complex, creating challenges for even the most knowledgeable person. Often, you will discover there is more than one way to accomplish a particular goal, and as a consequence the tax impact may be radically different, depending upon how you structure the transaction.

▶ *TAX TIP*

In most cases, the opportunities available to save or defer income taxes arise at the preliminary stage, before you have completed the proposed transaction. The manner in which a transaction is structured may also affect the GST payable. Having your tax adviser review what you have done after you have completed the arrangement is usually too late. The only way to take advantage of the rules is to conduct your tax planning well in advance.

127. REVENUE CANADA'S POLICY AND WHAT'S REALLY LAW

In most cases, amendments to the Income Tax Act are presented to the House of Commons as part of a budget. The Department of Finance, under the direction of the Minister of Finance, prepares these amendments. Once the amendments become law, Revenue Canada, Taxation — a separate department under the direction of the Minister of National Revenue — administers them.

Over the years, Revenue Canada has developed many administrative rules in an effort to deal with practical problems that always seem to pop up, and the apparent uncertainty in many areas of tax law. In some cases, the administrative rules may not even agree with the law.

In tax planning, you should know whether your plan complies with the tax law or whether it depends on Revenue Canada's stated policy. Revenue Canada is not bound by its stated policy, and the courts do not necessarily consider this policy in making their decisions.

128. T4s, T5s AND OTHER INFORMATION SLIPS

Any employment, pension and most investment income that you receive in 1998 is reported on information slips prepared by the person or organization that paid you. These slips must be mailed or delivered to you by February 28, 1999.

If you are a beneficiary of a trust, depending upon the year-end of the trust, your T3 information slip could be delayed until the end of March. Partnerships in which all of the members are individuals are required to file a partnership information return and issue the required information slips to the partners by March 31, 1999 **(see article 3)**.

Whether or not you receive the appropriate slip, you must declare all your income. Be sure to check the amounts reported on the slips to ensure they are correct, as mistakes on these documents are not uncommon. If there is an error, you can obtain an amended slip. If you are filing your tax return on paper, do not file it until all the necessary receipts and slips are in your hands. Otherwise, processing delays could result. Nevertheless, you should do everything possible to ensure that you do not file late.

If you are filing your return electronically **(see article 129)**, or using TELEFILE **(see article 130)**, all information slips must be retained in case Revenue Canada requests confirmation of the amount claimed. Your return will be reassessed if you cannot provide a copy of the relevant slip.

129. ELECTRONIC FILING OF TAX RETURNS

Electronic filing (EFILE) is a system that allows authorized persons to send personal income tax returns directly to Revenue Canada over the telephone lines. Since returns are received and verified almost instantly, refunds can often be issued within a couple of weeks of submitting your return.

Revenue Canada is currently working on a redesign of the corporate income tax system to facilitate the electronic filing of corporate income tax returns. Under the redesigned system, current forms and schedules will be revised and renumbered, and a uniform system of reporting financial information will be introduced — the General Index of Financial Information ("GIFI").

The GIFI is an index of items commonly found on income statements, balance sheets and statements of retained earnings. Financial information will be submitted to Revenue Canada using this standard codified index, which will have to be used in order to EFILE a corpo-rate tax return. The new system is scheduled to be in place in the fall of 1998.

130. REVENUE CANADA INTRODUCES TELEFILE

A new telephone-based system for filing individual income tax returns called TELEFILE has been introduced by Revenue Canada. It differs from the EFILE system in that taxpayers will be able to transmit income tax information themselves by way of telephone. TELEFILE is available in all provinces and territories but only to eligible taxpayers.

You need an invitation

Qualified taxpayers receive an invitation to participate when they receive their personalized income tax packages — for example, for 1997 income tax returns, eligible users were limited to wage earners, stu-dents, seniors, and credit and benefit filers. The invitation includes a TELEFILE access code, instructions and a remittance form. Taxpayers who do not receive an invitation with their package will not be able to use this service.

Tax return copy still needed

TELEFILE does not eliminate the need to complete a copy of the tax return. Taxpayers will enter tax data from a completed income tax return using their telephone keypad. On completion of the automated telephone interview, Revenue Canada will issue a confirmation number. A Notice of Assessment will usually be sent out within two weeks. Tax-payers are not required to file the supporting documentation used to prepare the return unless requested to do so.

131. NOTICE OF ASSESSMENT AND YOUR RETURN

Within a few months of filing your 1998 return, you should receive a Notice of Assessment from Revenue Canada. When you receive it, compare it to the taxes payable as reported on your return. If there is any discrepancy, try to determine the reason.

If you do not understand why the amounts are different or disagree with the assessment, consult your tax adviser or ask Revenue Canada to provide further details. Do not automatically assume you made the error. The assessment may be based upon a misunderstanding of the facts, or Revenue Canada quite possibly may have made an error in processing your return.

Reassessments and notices of objection

As a matter of policy, Revenue Canada will reassess returns if the adjustment relates to an error in arithmetic or a misunderstanding of the facts. If your dispute is based upon a different interpretation of the law, you have to file a notice of objection.

Taxpayers can initiate the appeal process by outlining the objection on Revenue Canada's form T400A, or by setting out the facts and reasons for their objection in a letter to the chief of appeals at their local Revenue Canada district office or taxation centre.

Generally, a Notice of Objection must be filed within 90 days of the mailing date of the Notice of Assessment. Individuals and testamentary trusts are granted a longer period of time to object to their assessment. They must object within one year from the filing due date of the return, or 90 days after the day of mailing the Notice of Assessment, whichever is later. Consult with your tax adviser if you believe a reassessment or an objection is warranted.

132. REVENUE CANADA'S COLLECTION PROCEDURES

If you cannot afford to pay taxes owing, you should know about Revenue Canada's collection procedures. Without a doubt, you should still file your return on time even if you are unable to pay the outstanding taxes. Filing late will incur a 5% penalty on the taxes owing, which is automatically added to the amount you owe.

An additional 1% is added for each additional complete month that the return is late, to a maximum of 12 months. Interest also accrues on the unpaid taxes. And if this is not your first late filing offence and a demand has been issued for you to file a return, you could be subject to a 10% penalty plus 2% per month for up to 20 months on the second late filed return. If you wilfully attempted to evade payment of income taxes by failing to file your return, additional penalties could apply.

What to expect

Normally, it takes Revenue Canada approximately six weeks to process and assess your return — less if you filed electronically or used TELE-FILE. The Notice of Assessment will show the amount of taxes owing including penalties and interest, and will state that no further interest will be charged if the entire amount is paid within 20 days.

If a payment is not made within 30 days, Revenue Canada will issue a request that the amount be paid. In most cases, Revenue Canada cannot begin legal proceedings to collect until 90 days after the date of assessment. There are further delays if you file a Notice of Objection. Nevertheless, the daily-compounded interest is charged and accumulates on the amount due from April 30 to the date of payment.

Subject to the restrictions relating to disputed amounts, Revenue Canada can seize funds from your bank account or require your employer to pay a portion of your salary directly towards your taxes owing.

Try to work out a payment schedule

Revenue Canada will make every effort to contact you before beginning formal legal proceedings, but it would be prudent for you to contact the department if you are unable to pay the full amount immediately. Depending on circumstances, Revenue Canada normally accepts a schedule of payments over a period of time.

133. INCOME TAX REFUNDS

You are eligible for an income tax refund if the amount of income taxes withheld from or paid by you during the year exceeds the actual taxes you owe. Although you may look forward to receiving a tax refund, it is not always good planning to get one. If you get a refund, that means Revenue Canada has been holding your money and not paying you interest on it for many months.

▶ *TAX TIP*

If you expect to receive a refund after filing your return — for example, due to RRSP contributions and other deductions — review the TD1 form you file with your employer and seek to have source withholdings reduced.

Requesting a refund for overpayment

Individuals and testamentary trusts may now claim a tax refund for taxation years as far back as 1985. For example, you may find that you failed to claim the "equivalent-to-married tax credit" **(see article 66)** in 1988 and 1989, even though you were entitled to do so. By writing a letter to the department, and including any supporting documents, you can request a refund.

Losing interest

Although you won't be penalized for filing a return late when you are owed a refund, interest does not begin to accrue on the refund amount until you file the return. For individual tax returns filed after 1992, interest on tax refunds does not start to accrue until 45 days after the balance-due date (April 30) or 45 days after the actual filing date — if it is later.

If you have made an error and you actually owe money, late filing penalties will apply on the balance owing. Therefore, regardless of whether you owe money or are receiving a refund, you should always file your return on time.

134. QUARTERLY INSTALMENTS

Historically, if you owe taxes each year when filing your return, there is a good chance you are required to prepay your tax through quarterly instalments. Failing to remit the instalments on time can be costly. Revenue Canada charges interest on the deficient amounts as if you owed the money and, if this interest charge adds up to more than $1,000, a charge of 50% of the interest in excess of $1,000 is added. This can become quite expensive and should be avoided if possible.

Instalments are due on March 15, June 15, September 15 and December 15. The rules used to determine when an individual is required to remit instalments cause difficulties for many taxpayers and changes to these rules introduced in 1994 have, regrettably, added further confusion. That's why it's so important to understand the requirement to make instalments and the options available to do so.

Instalment rules

Instalments are required if the difference between your combined federal and provincial tax and the amount of tax actually withheld at source was greater than $2,000 in either 1996 or 1997, and will be greater than $2,000 in 1998. This last test requires an estimate in advance of the actual calculation of 1998 tax.

Once it is determined that you are required to make 1998 instalment payments, you can choose from three options to calculate the amount of your instalment.

Under the first two options, you can base your instalments on your 1997 tax, or base them on your estimate of your 1998 tax. If you choose the latter option, be careful. Underestimating your 1998 tax means Revenue Canada will charge you interest based on the higher instalment required.

Revenue Canada calculations

With the third option, Revenue Canada calculates the amount of your instalment and sends you the calculation as a reminder. Revenue Canada initiated this option to eliminate some of the confusion in this area. Unfortunately, the calculation notices look very much like requests to pay and have created confusion for many taxpayers.

This method uses 1996 as the base for the first two instalments. For the last two instalments, the amounts are based on the 1997 tax, less whatever was required for the first two instalments. The final result will be total instalments equal to 1997 tax.

The major advantage in paying the amounts shown on the Revenue Canada notices is that you will not be charged any instalment interest if you pay on time. Revenue Canada sends the instalment reminders in batches of two — in February, for the March and June instalments, and in August, for the September and December instalments.

▶ *TAX TIP*

If you discover during the year that you should have been making higher instalments, it is possible to catch up because Revenue Canada will credit interest on overpayments and apply that against interest deficiencies. For instance, if you remit $5,000 on March 15 and then discover just before the June 15 deadline that you should be remitting $6,000 each quarter, it would be prudent for you to remit $8,000 on June 15, $5,000 on September 15 and

$6,000 on December 15. The end result will be that you were $1,000 short for the three months from March 15 to June 15 and $1,000 over for the next three months. The interest calculations for these two periods will offset each other, assuming the prescribed interest rate does not change over that period.

135. DIRECTOR'S LIABILITY

As a director of a corporation, you should be aware of your responsibility should the corporation fail to deduct and remit income taxes on payments to employees or on certain payments to non-residents. Directors can also be held liable for failure of the corporation to collect and remit GST.

Should the corporation fail to deduct and remit, you can be liable along with the corporation for paying the required amounts, including interest and penalties. However, you will not be held liable if you can demonstrate that you exercised a reasonable degree of care to prevent the failure of withholding and remitting.

Nevertheless, there have been several court cases where directors have been found liable. Often the moneylender cuts off the line of credit to the business and, as a result, the withholding cannot be paid. Since the withholding is supposed to be in a trust account, this excuse is generally not sufficient to protect you from liability. As you might expect, ignorance is not an acceptable defence.

> ▶ *TAX TIP*
> Do not take your responsibility as a director lightly. If the corporation is in financial difficulty, you should take additional precautions to ensure that withholding taxes are remitted on a timely basis.

136. BE AWARE OF PENALTIES AND INTEREST

The concept of increased penalties for repeat offenders is now firmly entrenched in the Income Tax Act.

The penalty for filing a return late is 5% of the unpaid taxes plus an additional 1% for each complete month the return is late, up to a maximum of 12 months — a maximum penalty of 17%.

Additionally, if you have been assessed this penalty for one or more of the three prior years and Revenue Canada issues a demand to file the current year's return, it's a good idea to comply. The penalty for a repeat offence will be 10% of the unpaid taxes plus an additional 2% per month for a period up to 20 months — a maximum penalty of 50% **(see article 132)**.

Similarly, if you fail to report an amount for a given year and then fail to report another amount in one or more of three subsequent years, a special penalty equal to 10% of the amount you failed to report the second time will apply.

And don't forget the additional penalties imposed for failing to make the appropriate amount of income tax instalments **(see article 134)**.

There are also penalties for failing to provide your SIN (social insurance number) or your BIN (business identification number) or for failing to include the SIN or BIN on an information slip that you have prepared **(see article 78)**. Partnerships and tax shelters are also subject to penalties for failure to file the required information returns.

Even bigger penalties

If you knowingly, or in circumstances amounting to gross negligence, make false statements or omit information from a return, a penalty of 50% of the tax that would otherwise have been incurred may be imposed. And if Revenue Canada finds that a false statement or omission amounts to tax evasion, a fine of 50% to 200% of the tax evaded may be imposed.

The interest rate charged on amounts owing to Revenue Canada is 2% higher than the rate Revenue Canada pays on refunds. The increased rate applies to all amounts owing to Revenue Canada including unpaid taxes, instalments and source deductions.

Voluntary disclosures

It is Revenue Canada's policy not to impose penalties when a voluntary disclosure is made. If a taxpayer has never filed tax returns, and the returns are then voluntarily filed, the taxpayer will be required to pay only the tax owing — with interest — on the reported incomes. If a taxpayer has given incomplete information in a return and subsequently submits the missing information, the taxpayer will be required to pay only the tax owing on the adjusted income, with interest.

In order to make a voluntary disclosure you have to initiate the disclosure. A disclosure is not considered voluntary if it arises when Revenue

Canada has begun an audit or a request for information has been issued. Contact your tax adviser regarding initial contact with Revenue Canada and the information to be provided.

Ministerial discretion to waive interest and penalties

In some cases, interest and penalties may have arisen due to no fault of your own. To deal with such inequities, there are rules that allow the minister to waive or cancel interest or penalties at any time starting with the 1985 taxation year.

For example, interest and penalties may be waived if you can show that you were prevented from filing on time due to extraordinary circumstances. These may include factors such as illness, death, natural disaster, disruption in services, or erroneous information from Revenue Canada in the form of incorrect written answers or errors in published information.

TAX CALENDAR

Payment and Filing Due Dates

Type of Return	Payment Due Date[1]	Filing Due Date
Individual income tax returns:		
Federal		
• general	April 30	April 30
• self-employed[2]	April 30	June 15
• deceased	April 30[3]	April 30/June 15[4]
Quebec		
• general	April 30	April 30
• self-employed[5]	April 30	June 15
• deceased	April 30[3]	April 30/June 15[4]
Corporate income tax returns:	End of:	End of:
Federal, Alberta, Ontario	2 months after *y/e[6]	6 months after y/e
Quebec	2 months after y/e	6 months after y/e
Corporate capital tax returns:	End of:	End of:
Federal[7]	2 months after y/e[6]	6 months after y/e
British Columbia	184 days after y/e[8]	184 days after y/e
Alberta[9]	2 months after y/e[6]	6 months after y/e
Saskatchewan	6 months after y/e	6 months after y/e
Manitoba	6 months after y/e[8]	6 months after y/e
Ontario[10]	2 months after y/e[6]	6 months after y/e
Quebec[10]	2 months after y/e	6 months after y/e
New Brunswick[11]	6 months after y/e	6 months after y/e
Prince Edward Island[9]	6 months after y/e	6 months after y/e
Nova Scotia[11]	6 months after y/e	6 months after y/e
Newfoundland[9]	6 months after y/e	6 months after y/e
Trust (estate) income tax returns:		
Federal	90 days after y/e	90 days after y/e
Quebec	90 days after y/e	90 days after y/e
Information returns:		
Partnership	N/A	March 31[12]
Tax shelter	N/A	Last day of February
Transactions with related non-residents	N/A	6 months after y/e
Foreign Holdings:		
Transfers/loans to non-resident trusts	N/A	Filing due date of taxpayer's income tax return for the year[13]

Distributions from non-resident trusts	N/A	Filing due date of tax-payer's income tax return or partnership's information return[14]
Interests in foreign affiliates	N/A	15 months after y/e
Specified foreign property	N/A	Filing due date of tax-payer's income tax return or partnership's information return[15]
Information Slips:		
T4, T5	N/A	Last day of February[16]
T3	N/A	90 days after y/e

* Note: (y/e means year-end)

[1]The date indicates the due date for the final payment of taxes for the year. Payments may be required throughout the year. Individuals, if required, make instalments of tax quarterly (i.e., March 15, June 15, September 15 and December 15). Corporations, if required, generally remit taxes monthly.

[2]The filing deadline applies to an individual who carried on business (other than a tax shelter investment) in the year, and his or her spouse.

[3]For deaths occurring before November 1 of the year. For deaths occurring during November and December of the year, tax is payable six months after the date of death. When the death occurs between January 1 and April 30, the tax payable for the prior year is due six months after the date of death. Quarterly instalments of tax are not required after the date of death.

[4]For deaths occurring before November 1 of the year, the return is due by the normal filing date, either April 30 or June 15. For deaths during the period beginning November 1 of the year and ending April 30 of the following year (or June 15 if the filing extension would have applied), the return is due by the later of six months after the date of death and the normal filing date.

[5]The province of Quebec adopts the federal due date for an individual reporting business income, and his or her spouse.

[6]End of third month following the y/e if the corporation is a Canadian controlled private corporation and :

Federal: the small business deduction is claimed in the current or preceding year, and the aggregate of taxable income of the corporation and all associated corporations for the immediately preceding year was $200,000 or less.

Alberta: the Alberta small business deduction is claimed in the year or immediately preceding year, and the corporation has taxable income of $500,000 or less in the year or preceding year.

Ontario: the corporation has taxable income for the preceding year of less than $200,000.

[7]Applies to Tax on Large Corporations and Financial Institutions Capital Tax. Separate capital tax returns are not required. Schedules are filed with the federal income tax return.

[8]Instalments, if required, are made quarterly. In the case of Manitoba - for fiscal periods beginning before January 1, 1998 - if capital tax for the preceding year was $1,200 or less, only one instalment of tax is due 15 days prior to the end of the fiscal period. For fiscal periods commencing after January 1, 1998, if capital tax for the preceding year was $2,400 or less, only one instalment of tax is due within three months following the end of the fiscal period. However, if instalments were not required in the preceding year and estimated taxes for the current year exceed $2,400 quarterly instalments will be required.

[9]Capital tax is levied on financial institutions. A separate tax return is required.

[10]Part of the corporate income tax return. A separate tax return is not required.

[11]Applies to capital tax on financial institutions. For other corporations, the Tax on Large Corporations, effective for taxation years ending after March 31, 1997, will be collected with the federal corporate tax return. A separate capital tax return is not required.

[12]If all members are individuals. If all members are corporations, the deadline is the last day of the fifth month following the fiscal year-end. For partnerships with mixed members, the earlier of these two dates. If the partnership discontinues its business or activity, the deadline is the earlier of 90 days after the discontinuance and the date the return would be required.

[13]Where a taxpayer has transferred or loaned funds or property at any time to a foreign based trust, the information return must be filed by the due date of the taxpayer's return for the particular year that includes the end of the trust's year before which a transfer was made, or during which the non-resident trust was indebted to the taxpayer.

[14]Where a taxpayer or partnership has received funds or property from or is indebted to a foreign-based trust, the information return must be filed by the due date of the taxpayer's return for the particular year during which the distribution was received or the taxpayer was indebted to the foreign trust. In case of a partnership, the information return must be filed by the due date of the partnership information return, whether or not one is required.

[15]Effective for taxation years and fiscal periods ending in 1998 and subsequent years; however, no return is due before April 30, 1999.

[16]Where the business activity is discontinued, the filing deadline is 30 days thereafter.

TABLES

Table 1
1998 Federal Tax Credits
This table shows the amounts you can claim as credits and the approximate tax savings that correspond to each.

Type of credit	($) Amount	Federal tax credit	Approximate tax saving(a)
Basic personal amount	$6,456	$1,098	$1,702
Supplementary personal (b)	$500	$85	$132
Supplementary personal with a dependant (c)	$1,000	$170	$264
Married amount (d)	$5,380	$915	$1,418
Infirm dependants 18 and over (e)	$2,353	$400	$620
Disability (f) & (g)	$4,233	$720	$1,116
Caregivers' amount (h)	$2,353	$400	$620
Age 65 or over (f) & (i)	$3,482	$592	$918
Pension income (f)	up to $1,000	17% (up to $170)	26.35% (up to $264)
Tuition fees (f) (j) & (k)	amount paid (minimum $100 per institution)	17%	26.35%
Education (f) (j) & (k)			
-full-time	$200/month	17%	26.35%
-part-time	$60/month	17%	26.35%
Medical expenses	amount over lesser of $1,614 and 3% of net income	17%	26.35%
Student loan interest	amount paid	17%	26.35%
Charitable donations (l)	up to 75% of net income	17% of first $200; 29% of excess	26.35% of first $200; 44.95% of excess
CPP and UI premiums	limited to maximum premium for the year	17%	26.35%

The unused portion of any tax credits is not refundable to individuals who otherwise have no tax to pay.

Notes:

a. Assumes provincial tax is approximately 55% of federal tax.

b. The amount eligible for the credit is reduced by 4% of income in excess of $6,956. Effective July 1998, therefore, the credit for 1998 is 50% of the amount shown.

c. The amount eligible for the credit is reduced by 4% of the amount by which the individual's net income exceeds the sum of $6,956 and the excess of $6,956 less the dependant's net income. If the dependant's net income is greater than $6,956, there will be no additional amount in respect of the dependant. The dependant must claim the supplementary personal amount on his or her own return. Credit for 1998 is 50% of the amount shown.

d. Amount claimed for spouse or equivalent-to-married credit for a related dependant (where there is no spouse). The value of the credit is reduced by 17% of spouse's (or dependant's) income in excess of $538.

e. The value of the credit is reduced by 17% of dependant's income in excess of $4,103.

f. The unused portion of the credit is transferable as follows:

Age and pension income — to spouse only (see article 69)

Tuition fees/education — to spouse or supporting parent or grandparent (see article 63)

Disability — to spouse or other supporting person

g. The taxpayer is not entitled to this amount if medical expenses for a full-time attendant or for care in a nursing home have been claimed.

h. The value of the credit is reduced by 17% of dependant's income in excess of $11,500.

i. The amount eligible for the credit (i.e., $3,482) is reduced by 15% of net income in excess of $25,921.

j. The maximum transferable tax credit is $850 (tuition fees and education credit combined).

k. Tuition and education amounts not fully used in the current year by the student and not transferred to an eligible person will be available for carryforward for the student's use in a subsequent year.

l. In the year of death, the limit may be raised to 100% of net income. As well, where capital property is donated to a charity, the limit is increased by 25% of any taxable capital gain plus 25% of recapture realized upon donating the property.

Table 2
1998 Federal Tax Rates

Taxable income	Income tax
$29,590 or less	17%
$29,590 to $59,180	$5,030 + 26% on next $29,590
Over $59,180	$12,724 + 29% on excess

Basic federal tax	Federal surtax
$12,500 or less	3% of basic federal tax (a)
Over $12,500	$375 + 8% of basic federal
	tax over $12,500

1998 Provincial Tax Rates
(percentage of federal tax)

British Columbia	50.5% (b)
Alberta	44.0% (c)
Saskatchewan	49.0% (d)
Manitoba	51.0% (e)
Ontario	42.75% (f)
Quebec	n/a (g)
New Brunswick	61.0% (h)
Prince Edward Island	59.5% (i)
Nova Scotia	57.5% (j)
Newfoundland	69.0% (k)
Northwest Territories	45.0%
Yukon	50.0% (l)

Notes:

a. Reduction in surtax = $250 less 6% of basic federal tax in excess of $8,333. For 1998, the reduction will be the lesser of: 50% of this amount and 50% of the surtax.

b. Surtax = 30% of basic B.C. tax in excess of $5,300 plus an additional 26.0% of basic B.C. tax in excess of $8,660.

c. Flat tax = 0.5% of Alta. taxable income; Surtax = 8% of basic Alta. tax in excess of $3,500.

d. Flat tax = 2% of net income; surtax = 15% of Sask. provincial tax (including flat tax) in excess of $4,000 plus an additional deficit surtax equal to 10% of Sask. basic and flat tax. There is up to a $150 reduction in deficit surtax for individual taxpayers depending upon income levels.

e. Flat tax = 2% of net income; surtax = 2% of net income in excess of $30,000.

f. Fair Share Health Care Levy = 20% of basic Ont. tax in excess of $4,057.50 plus an additional 33% of basic Ont. tax in excess of $5,217.50.

g. Que. has its own personal tax system which requires a separate calculation of taxable income. Tax rates range from 0% to 26.0%.

h. Surtax = 8% of basic N.B. tax in excess of $13,500.

i. Surtax = 10% of basic P.E.I. tax in excess of $5,200.

j. Surtax = 10% of basic N.S. tax in excess of $10,000.

k. Surtax = 10% of basic Nfld. Tax in excess of $7,900.

l. Surtax = 5% of basic Yukon tax in excess of $6,000.

Table 3

Estimate of Income Taxes Payable (1998)

(residents of provinces other than Quebec)

Taxable income	$_____(A)
Federal taxes payable	
Taxable income(A)	
If less than $29,590: _____(A) x 17%	$_____(B)
If $29,590 to $59,180: _____(A) - $29,590 x 26% + $5,030	_____(C)
Over $59,180 _____(A) - $59, 180 x 29% + $12, 724	_____(D)
Total federal tax credits from Table 1	_____(E)
13.33% of taxable dividends	_____(F)
Basic federal tax (B), (C) or (D) - [(E) + (F)]	_____(G)
Foreign tax credit	_____(H)
Federal tax (G − H)	_____(I)
Federal surtax:	
Regular _____(G) X 3%	_____(J)
Reduction [$250 − 6% (___(G) - $8,333)] x 50%	_____(K)
Reduction limitation (J X 50%)	_____(L)
Surtax reduction: lesser of (K) and (L)	_____(M)
High income _____(G) - $12,500 x 5%	_____(N)
Total federal tax (I) + (J)- (M) + (N)	_____(O)
Provincial taxes payable	
Basic provincial tax: _____(G) x provincial rate (Table 2)	_____(P)
Provincial flat tax: _____(A) x rate (Table 2)	_____(Q)
Provincial surtax: _____(P) - base amount x rate (Table 2)	_____(R)
Total provincial tax (P) + (Q) + (R)	_____(S)
Total tax (O) + (S)	

Note:

For purposes of calculating provincial flat taxes for residents of Manitoba and Saskatchewan, it has been assumed that net income is equal to taxable income.

For Manitoba, the provincial surtax is based on net income rather than basic provincial tax. Therefore, the provincial surtax calculation for residents of Manitoba is [(A) - $30,000] x 2%.

Table 4
1998 Top Marginal Rates of Tax
(federal and provincial combined)

Province	Interest & foreign dividends (%)	Canadian dividends (%)	Capital gains (%)
British Columbia	54.17	36.58	40.63
Alberta	45.60	31.08	34.20
Saskatchewan	51.58	36.27	38.69
Manitoba	50.11	36.14	37.58
Ontario	50.29	33.96	37.72
Quebec	52.61	39.39	39.46
New Brunswick	50.43	34.05	37.82
Prince Edward Island	50.30	33.97	37.73
Nova Scotia	49.66	33.54	37.25
Newfoundland	53.33	36.01	40.00
Northwest Territories	44.37	29.96	33.28
Yukon	46.55	31.43	34.91

Note:
Interest and foreign dividends are taxed in the same way as most income. Canadian dividends are subject to a gross-up and a tax credit, producing a lower tax burden. Capital gains receive favourable treatment because only three-quarters of capital gains are taxed (at the same rate as interest).

Table 5
Tax Payable at Various Levels of Taxable Income (a)

Taxable income ($)	British Columbia tax ($)	percentage (%)*	Alberta tax ($)	percentage (%)*
20, 000	3, 500	25.8	3, 450	25.2
22, 000	4, 017	25.8	3, 955	25.2
24, 000	4, 533	25.8	4, 460	25.2
26, 000	5, 050	25.8	4, 964	25.2
28, 000	5, 567	25.8	5, 469	25.2
29, 590	5, 977	39.5	5, 870	38.3
30, 000	6, 139	39.5	6, 027	38.3
32, 000	6, 930	39.5	6, 793	38.3

*see note (b)

Taxable income ($)	British Columbia tax ($)	percentage (%)*	Alberta tax ($)	percentage (%)*
34, 000	7, 720	39.5	7, 560	38.3
36, 000	8, 511	39.5	8, 327	38.3
38, 000	9, 301	39.5	9, 093	38.3
40, 000	10, 091	39.5	9, 860	38.3
42, 000	10, 882	39.5	10, 626	38.3
44, 000	11, 672	39.5	11, 393	38.8
46, 000	12, 463	40.4	12, 168	40.1
48, 000	13, 270	40.7	12, 971	40.4
50, 000	14, 084	40.7	13, 779	40.4
52, 000	14, 898	40.7	14, 587	40.4
54, 000	15, 712	43.0	15, 395	40.4
56, 000	16, 572	44.6	16, 204	40.4
58, 000	17, 464	44.7	17, 012	40.5
59, 180	17, 992	49.8	17, 490	45.0
60, 000	18, 400	49.8	17, 859	45.0
62, 000	19, 396	50.3	18, 759	45.5
64, 000	20, 402	50.4	19, 670	45.6
66, 000	21, 409	50.4	20, 582	45.6
68, 000	22, 416	50.4	21, 494	45.6
70, 000	23, 423	50.4	22, 406	45.6
75, 000	25, 941	51.7	24, 686	45.6
80, 000	28, 527	54.2	26, 966	45.6
85, 000	31, 235	54.2	29, 247	45.6
90, 000	33, 943	54.2	31, 527	45.6
95, 000	36, 652	54.2	33, 807	45.6
100, 000	39, 360	54.2	36, 087	45.6
105, 000	42, 068	54.2	38, 367	45.6
110, 000	44, 777	54.2	40, 647	45.6
115, 000	47, 485	54.2	42, 927	45.6
120, 000	50, 193	54.2	45, 207	45.6
125, 000	52, 902	54.2	47, 487	45.6
150, 000	66, 443	54.2	58, 887	45.6
250, 000	120, 609	54.2	104, 488	45.6
500, 000	256, 025	54.2	218, 490	45.6

* see note (b)

Taxable income ($)	Saskatchewan tax ($)	percentage (%)*	Manitoba tax ($)	percentage (%)*
20, 000	3, 868	28.6	3, 911	27.9
22, 000	4, 440	28.6	4, 470	27.9
24, 000	5, 013	28.6	5, 028	27.9
26, 000	5, 585	28.6	5, 587	27.9
28, 000	6, 157	28.6	6, 145	27.9
29, 590	6, 612	42.6	6, 589	41.7
30, 000	6, 787	42.6	6, 760	43.7
32, 000	7, 639	42.6	7, 633	43.7
34, 000	8, 491	42.6	8, 506	43.7
36, 000	9, 343	42.6	9, 379	43.7
38, 000	10, 195	43.0	10, 252	43.7
40, 000	11, 055	44.8	11, 125	43.7
42, 000	11, 951	44.8	11, 998	43.7
44, 000	12, 848	44.8	12, 871	43.7
46, 000	13, 744	45.7	13, 744	44.5
48, 000	14, 658	46.0	14, 634	44.8
50, 000	15, 577	46.0	15, 530	44.8
52, 000	16, 497	46.0	16, 427	44.8
54, 000	17, 417	46.0	17, 323	44.8
56, 000	18, 336	46.0	18, 220	44.8
58, 000	19, 256	46.1	19, 116	44.9
59, 180	19, 800	51.0	19, 646	49.5
60, 000	20, 218	51.0	20, 052	49.5
62, 000	21, 238	51.6	21, 043	50.1
64, 000	22, 269	51.6	22, 044	50.1
66, 000	23, 300	51.6	23, 046	50.1
68, 000	24, 332	51.6	24, 048	50.1
70, 000	25, 364	51.6	25, 050	50.1
75, 000	27, 943	51.6	27, 556	50.1
80, 000	30, 522	51.6	30, 061	50.1
85, 000	33, 101	51.6	32, 567	50.1
90, 000	35, 680	51.6	35, 072	50.1
95, 000	38, 259	51.6	37, 578	50.1
100, 000	40, 838	51.6	40, 083	50.1
105, 000	43, 417	51.6	42, 589	50.1
110, 000	45, 997	51.6	45, 094	50.1

Taxable income ($)	Saskatchewan tax ($)	percentage (%)*	Manitoba tax ($)	percentage (%)*
115, 000	48, 576	51.6	47, 600	50.1
120, 000	51, 155	51.6	50, 105	50.1
125, 000	53, 734	51.6	52, 611	50.1
150, 000	66, 630	51.6	65, 138	50.1
250, 000	118, 212	51.6	115, 248	50.1
500, 000	247, 168	51.6	240, 523	50.1

Taxable income ($)	Ontario tax ($)	percentage (%)*	Quebec (c) tax ($)	percentage (%)*
20, 000	3, 321	24.5	4, 065	34.5
22, 000	3, 812	24.5	4, 755	34.5
24, 000	4, 302	24.5	5, 445	34.5
26, 000	4, 793	24.5	6, 166	37.5
28, 000	5, 283	24.5	6, 916	37.5
29, 590	5, 673	37.3	7, 513	45.2
30, 000	5, 826	37.5	7, 698	45.2
32, 000	6, 576	37.5	8, 601	45.2
34, 000	7, 327	37.5	9, 505	45.2
36, 000	8, 077	37.5	10, 408	45.2
38, 000	8, 827	37.5	11, 311	45.2
40, 000	9, 577	37.5	12, 215	45.2
42, 000	10, 327	37.5	13, 118	45.2
44, 000	11, 077	37.5	14, 021	45.2
46, 000	11, 827	38.4	14, 925	45.7
48, 000	12, 595	38.7	15, 846	46.3
50, 000	13, 368	39.8	16, 772	49.4
52, 000	14, 165	40.9	17, 759	49.4
54, 000	14, 983	40.9	18, 746	49.4
56, 000	15, 800	40.9	19, 733	49.4
58, 000	16, 618	41.0	20, 720	49.4
59, 180	17, 102	45.6	21, 303	52.0
60, 000	17, 476	47.3	21, 729	52.0
62, 000	18, 422	50.2	22, 770	52.0
64, 000	19, 427	50.3	23, 821	52.0
66, 000	20, 433	50.3	24, 873	52.6
68, 000	21, 438	50.3	25, 925	52.6

Taxable income ($)	Ontario tax ($)	percentage (%)*	Quebec (c) tax ($)	percentage (%)*
70, 000	22, 444	50.3	26, 978	52.6
75, 000	24, 959	50.3	29, 608	52.6
80, 000	27, 473	50.3	32, 239	52.6
85, 000	29, 987	50.3	34, 870	52.6
90, 000	32, 502	50.3	37, 500	52.6
95, 000	35, 016	50.3	40, 131	52.6
100, 000	37, 531	50.3	42, 762	52.6
105, 000	40, 045	50.3	45, 392	52.6
110, 000	42, 559	50.3	48, 023	52.6
115, 000	45, 074	50.3	50, 654	52.6
120, 000	47, 588	50.3	53, 284	52.6
125, 000	50, 103	50.3	55, 915	52.6
150, 000	62, 675	50.3	69, 068	52.6
250, 000	112, 963	50.3	121, 681	52.6
500, 000	238, 683	50.3	253, 214	52.6

Taxable income ($)	New Brunswick tax ($)	percentage (%)*	Prince Edward Island tax ($)	percentage (%)*
20, 000	3, 742	27.6	3, 707	27.4
22, 000	4, 294	27.6	4, 254	27.4
24, 000	4, 847	27.6	4, 802	27.4
26, 000	5, 399	27.6	5, 349	27.4
28, 000	5, 952	27.6	5, 897	27.4
29, 590	6, 390	42.3	6, 331	41.9
30, 000	6, 564	42.3	6, 503	41.9
32, 000	7, 409	42.3	7, 340	41.9
34, 000	8, 254	42.3	8, 177	41.9
36, 000	9, 099	42.3	9, 015	41.9
38, 000	9, 944	42.3	9, 852	41.9
40, 000	10, 789	42.3	10, 689	41.9
42, 000	11, 634	42.3	11, 526	41.9
44, 000	12, 479	42.3	12, 363	41.9
46, 000	13, 324	43.1	13, 201	42.7
48, 000	14, 186	43.4	14, 055	44.5
50, 000	15, 054	43.4	14, 945	44.6
52, 000	15, 923	43.4	15, 837	44.6
54, 000	16, 791	43.4	16, 728	44.6

Taxable income ($)	New Brunswick tax ($)	percentage (%)*	Prince Edward Island tax ($)	percentage (%)*
56, 000	17, 659	43.4	17, 620	44.6
58, 000	18, 528	43.5	18, 512	44.7
59, 180	19, 041	48.4	19, 039	49.7
60, 000	19, 438	48.4	19, 446	49.7
62, 000	20, 407	49.0	20, 441	50.2
64, 000	21, 386	49.0	21, 446	50.3
66, 000	22, 366	49.0	22, 452	50.3
68, 000	23, 346	49.0	23, 458	50.3
70, 000	24, 327	49.0	24, 464	50.3
75, 000	26, 777	49.0	26, 979	50.3
80, 000	29, 228	49.0	29, 494	50.3
85, 000	31, 678	49.0	32, 009	50.3
90, 000	34, 129	49.0	34, 524	50.3
95, 000	36, 579	50.3	37, 039	50.3
100, 000	39, 095	50.4	39, 554	50.3
105, 000	41, 616	50.4	42, 069	50.3
110, 000	44, 137	50.4	44, 584	50.3
115, 000	46, 658	50.4	47, 099	50.3
120, 000	49, 180	50.4	49, 614	50.3
125, 000	51, 701	50.4	52, 129	50.3
150, 000	64, 307	50.4	64, 704	50.3
250, 000	114, 732	50.4	115, 005	50.3
500, 000	240, 795	50.4	240, 756	50.3

Taxable income ($)	Nova Scotia tax ($)	percentage (%)*	Newfoundland tax ($)	percentage (%)*
20, 000	3, 611	26.7	3, 926	29.0
22, 000	4, 202	27.0	4, 505	29.0
24, 000	4, 742	27.0	5, 085	29.0
26, 000	5, 283	27.0	5, 665	29.0
28, 000	5, 823	27.0	6, 245	29.0
29, 590	6, 253	41.3	6, 705	44.3
30, 000	6, 422	41.3	6, 887	44.3
32, 000	7, 249	41.3	7, 773	44.3
34, 000	8, 076	41.3	8, 660	44.3
36, 000	8, 903	41.3	9, 546	44.3

Taxable income ($)	Nova Scotia tax ($)	percentage (%)*	Newfoundland tax ($)	percentage (%)*
38, 000	9, 729	41.3	10, 433	44.3
40, 000	10, 556	41.3	11, 320	44.3
42, 000	11, 383	41.3	12, 206	44.3
44, 000	12, 210	41.3	13, 093	44.3
46, 000	13, 037	42.2	13, 979	45.2
48, 000	13, 881	42.5	14, 883	45.5
50, 000	14, 731	42.5	15, 793	45.5
52, 000	15, 581	42.5	16, 703	45.5
54, 000	16, 431	42.5	17, 613	45.5
56, 000	17, 282	42.5	18, 523	45.5
58, 000	18, 132	42.6	19, 433	46.6
59, 180	18, 634	47.4	19, 984	52.8
60, 000	19, 023	47.4	20, 416	52.8
62, 000	19, 971	47.9	21, 471	53.3
64, 000	20, 930	48.0	22, 537	53.3
66, 000	21, 890	48.0	23, 603	53.3
68, 000	22, 850	48.0	24, 670	53.3
70, 000	23, 810	48.0	25, 737	53.3
75, 000	26, 210	48.3	28, 403	53.3
80, 000	28, 625	49.7	31, 070	53.3
85, 000	31, 108	49.7	33, 736	53.3
90, 000	33, 591	49.7	36, 403	53.3
95, 000	36, 074	49.7	39, 069	53.3
100, 000	38, 558	49.7	41, 736	53.3
105, 000	41, 041	49.7	44, 402	53.3
110, 000	43, 524	49.7	47, 069	53.3
115, 000	46, 007	49.7	49, 735	53.3
120, 000	48, 490	49.7	52, 402	53.3
125, 000	50, 973	49.7	55, 069	53.3
150, 000	63, 389	49.7	68, 401	53.3
250, 000	113, 051	49.7	121, 732	53.3
500, 000	237, 208	49.7	255, 060	53.3

Notes:

a. This table shows the amount of tax payable for a given taxable income by a person whose only tax credit is the basic non-refundable personal credit and who has no income from taxable Canadian dividends. Taxable income is assumed to be equal to net income.

b. The marginal rate of tax is the average rate applicable to each additional $1 of income within the interval indicated on the table.

c. Quebec's tax system is significantly different from those of the other provinces, and the amounts listed are illustrative rather than exact calculations. Allowable deductions will generally make taxable income somewhat lower for a resident of Quebec than for a resident elsewhere in Canada with the same total income.

In addition, beginning in the 1998 taxation year, individuals other than trusts will be able to choose between the general tax system and a new, simplified income tax system. Opting for the simplified tax system, individuals will replace a number of tax credits and deductions with a lump-sum non-refundable credit of $541 per taxpayer. Under this new system, spouses will also be able to file a joint return if they wish. The ministère du Revenu du Québec will indicate to the taxpayers whether it will be advantageous for them to use the simplified system.

Table 6
Canada Pension Plan Contributions and Benefits (1998)

Contributions:

Pensionable earnings	$36, 900
Year's basic exemption	$3, 500
Maximum contributory earnings	$33, 400
Employee and employer rate	3.2%
Maximum annual employee/employer contribution	$1, 068.80
Maximum annual self-employed contribution	$2, 137.60

Benefits:

Maximum monthly pension:	
if starting at age 60	$521.35
if starting at age 65	$744.79
if starting at age 70	$968.23
Maximum single payment on death	$2, 500.00
Maximum monthly pension for surviving spouse:	
under 65 years of age	$410.70
65 years of age and over	$446.87
Maximum monthly disability pension	$895.36

Notes:

a. Persons over 60 years of age are eligible to receive pension benefits. The pension amount is reduced before age 65 or increased after age 65 by 1/2 of 1% (or 6% per year) for each month between the beneficiary's 65th birthday and the month the pension becomes payable. The contributor has the option of drawing retirement benefits as early as age 60 or as late as age 70.

b. When the surviving spouse reaches 65, the pension is equal to 60% of the retirement pension. The pension will continue to be paid even if the surviving spouse remarries.

c. Married individuals may apply to have up to 50% of their CPP retirement benefits assigned to their spouses if the spouse is at least 60 years old (see article 76). CPP credits may also be divided on application by a legal spouse or common-law spouse after a separation of at least one year.

Table 7
Employment Insurance (1998)

Maximum insurable earnings	$39, 000.00
Employee rate	2.70%
Maximum employee premiums	$1, 053.00
Employer rate	3.78%
Maximum employer premiums	$1, 474.20
Maximum weekly benefits	$413.00

Repayment of Employment Insurance (EI) benefits

You must repay a percentage of your EI benefits if your net income for the year exceeds a threshold amount. The repayment is 30% of the amount by which your net income exceeds the threshold amounts indicated below:

a. $48,750 if: (i) you have 20 or fewer weeks of EI benefits in your claims history from the previous year; or (ii) the only benefits you received in the latest taxation year are maternity, parental or sickness benefits.

b. $39,000 if you have more than 20 weeks of EI benefits in your claims history. Note: only regular benefits are counted.

The amount repayable will be subject to a maximum, ranging from 30% to 100% of the benefits received, depending on your claim history.

The repayment must be included in your income tax return as taxes payable. The amount of the repayment is deductible in computing net income for the year.

Non-insurable employment:

- employment by a corporation of a person who owns more than 40% of the issued voting shares;
- certain non-arm's-length employment;
- casual employment, if it is not for your usual trade or business.

Table 8
1998 Federal Corporate Income Tax Rates

Income eligible for the small business deduction	13.12
Active business income not eligible for the small business deduction – manufacturing and processing profits earned in Canada	22.12
Active business income not eligible for the small business deduction – other business income	29.12
Income not from an active business (CCPC)(a)	29.12

Note:

a. A refundable tax of 6 2/3% is imposed on investment income of a CCPC. This tax is in addition to the taxes outlined above and will be included as a portion of the taxes that may be refunded to a corporation on the payment of a taxable dividend.

1998 Provincial Corporate Tax Rates

	SBD only	M&P only	Other Income
British Columbia	0% Or 9% (a)	16.5%	16.5%
Alberta	6%	14.5%	15.5%
Saskatchewan	8%	10%	17%
Manitoba	9%	17%	17%
Ontario	9.0% - 9.5% (b)(c)	13.5% (d)	15.5%
Quebec	0% or 5.9% (e)(f)	9.1%	9.1% or 16.71% (g)
New Brunswick	7%	17%	17%
Prince Edward Island	7.5%	7.5%	16% (h)
Nova Scotia	0% or 5% (i)	16%	16%
Newfoundland (j)	5%	5%	14%
Northwest Territories	5%	14%	14%
Yukon	2.5% or 6% (k)	2.5%	15%

In addition to income tax, a tax on capital is levied in Saskatchewan, Manitoba, New Brunswick, Nova Scotia, Ontario, and Quebec. Alberta, British Columbia, Prince Edward Island and Newfoundland levy a tax on capital on banks and trust and loan companies.

Notes:

a. B.C. - There is a two-year corporate income tax holiday for eligible new small businesses incorporated after April 30, 1996, and before April 1, 2001.

b. Ontario's small business corporate income tax rate is to be reduced to 9.0% from 9.5%, effective May 5, 1998, with proration for taxation years that straddle that date.

c. An Ontario surtax is levied on corporations claiming the Ontario small business deduction. The surtax is equal to the lesser of 4% of taxable income in excess of $200,000, and the Ontario small business deduction claimed. The effect is to recover the entire small business deduction once taxable income reaches $500,000.

d. This rate also applies to income derived from mining, logging, farming or fishing activities.

e. Companies incorporated after May 1, 1986, which are carrying on an eligible business, are exempt from paying income tax for their first three taxation years. For companies incorporated after March 25, 1997, this exemption will be for the first five taxation years.

f. The low rate is applicable for corporations whose taxable capital for Quebec tax purposes is less than $10 million.

g. Non-active business income is taxed at 16.71%.

h. PEI's corporate income tax rate increased to 16% from 15% effective July 1, 1997, with proration for taxation years that straddle that date.

i. Newly incorporated small businesses are not subject to any tax on income qualifying for the small business deduction for their first three taxation years.

j. A ten-year provincial tax holiday can apply for qualified new and expanding businesses in the province.

k. The rate for manufacturing income is 2.5% and the rate for non-manufacturing income is 6%.

Offices

Grant Thornton offices are located across Canada. We invite you to contact any of our offices directly either by the address and phone numbers listed below, or by e-mail using the following formula: office@GrantThornton.ca. For example, you can send e-mail to our Sault Ste. Marie office at saultstemarie@GrantThornton.ca.

NATIONAL OFFICE

Tenth Floor, North Tower
Royal Bank Plaza
200 Bay Street, Box 55
Toronto Ont. M5J 2P9

Telephone:
(416) 366-0100
Facsimile:
(416) 360-4944

Halifax Site:
2000 Barrington Street
Suite 500
Cogswell Tower
P.O. Box 426
Halifax, N.S. B3J 2P8

Telephone:
(902) 421-1734
1-800-424-8296
Facsimile:
(902) 421-1677

AMHERST, N.S.

134 Victoria Street East
P.O. Box 217
B4H 3Z2

Telephone:
(902) 667-3833
Facsimile:
(902) 667-0884

ANTIGONISH, N.S

257 Main Street
P.O. Box 1480
B2G 2L7

Telephone:
(902) 863-4587
Facsimile:
(902) 863-0917

BATHURST, N.B.

275 Main Street
Suite 500
P.O. Box 220
E2A 3Z2

Telephone:
(506) 546-6616
Facsimile:
(506) 548-5622

BRIDGEWATER, N.S.
166 North Street
P.O. Box 220
B4V 2V6

Telephone:
(902) 543-8115
Facsimile:
(902) 543-7707

CALGARY, Alta.
Suite 1900
500 - 4th Avenue SW
T2P 2V6

Telephone:
(403) 260-2500
Facsimile:
(403) 260-2571

CHARLOTTETOWN, P.E.I.
199 Grafton Street
Suite 501
P.O. Box 187
C1A 7K4

Telephone:
(902) 892-6547
Facsimile:
(902) 566-5358

CORNER BROOK, Nfld.
49-51 Park Street
P.O. Box 356
A2H 6E3

Telephone:
(709) 634-4382
Facsimile:
(709) 634-9158

DARTMOUTH, N.S.
44 Portland Street
Suite 301
P.O. Box 933
B2Y 3Z6

Telephone:
(902) 463-4900
Facsimile:
(902) 469-2860

DIGBY, N.S.
Basin Place
68 Water Street
P.O. Box 848
B0V 1A0

Telephone:
(902) 245-2553
Facsimile:
(902) 245-6161

EDMONTON, Alta.

2400 Scotia Place	Telephone:
10060 Jasper Avenue	(403) 422-7114
T5J 3R8	Facsimile:
	(403) 426-3208

FREDERICTON, N.B.

570 Queen Street	Telephone:
Suite 500	(506) 458-8200
P.O. Box 1054	Facsimile:
E3B 5C2	(506) 453-7029

GRAND FALLS - WINDSOR, Nfld.

9 High Street	Telephone:
P.O. Box 83	(709) 489-6622
A2A 2J3	Facsimile:
	(709) 489-6625

HALIFAX, N.S.

2000 Barrington Street	Telephone:
Suite 1100, Cogswell Tower	(902) 421-1734
P.O. Box 426	Facsimile:
B3J 2P8	(902) 420-1068

HAMILTON, Ont.

Suite 1040	Telephone:
Standard Life Centre	(905) 525-1930
120 King Street West	Facsimile:
L8P 4V2	(905) 527-4413

KELOWNA, B.C.

247 Lawrence Avenue	Telephone:
V1Y 6L2	(250) 762-4434
	Facsimile:
	(250) 762-8896

KENTVILLE, N.S.
15 Webster Street
P.O. Box 68
B4N 3V9

Telephone:
(902) 678-7307
Facsimile:
(902) 679-1870

LONDON, Ont.
389 Hyde Park Road
N6H 3R8

Telephone:
(519) 473-1160
Facsimile:
(519) 657-4450

MARKHAM, Ont.
7030 Woodbine Avenue
Suite 400
L3R 6G2

Telephone:
(905) 475-1100
Facsimile:
(905) 475-8906

MARYSTOWN, Nfld.
2 Queen Street
P.O. Box 518
A0E 2M0

Telephone:
(709) 279-2300
Facsimile:
(709) 279-2340

MIRAMICHI , N.B.
135 Henry Street
E1V 2N5

Telephone:
(506) 622-0637
Facsimile:
(506) 622-5174

MISSISSAUGA, Ont.
10 Kingsbridge Garden
Circle
Suite 400
L5R 3K6

Telephone:
(905) 568-4260
Facsimile:
(905) 568-4310

MONCTON, N.B.
Suite 500, 633 Main
P.O. Box 1005
E1C 8P2

Telephone:
(506) 857-0100
Facsimile:
(506) 857-0105

NEW GLASGOW, N.S.
610 East River Road
P.O. Box 427
B2H 5E5

Telephone:
(902) 752-8393
Facsimile:
(902) 752-4009

NEW LISKEARD, Ont.
17 Wellington Street
P.O. Box 2170
P0J 1P0

Telephone:
(705) 647-8100
Facsimile:
(705) 647-7026

NEW WESTMINSTER, B.C.
604 Columbia Street
4th Floor
V3M 1A6

Telephone:
(604) 521-3761
Facsimile:
(604) 521-8170

NORTH BAY, Ont.
222 McIntyre Street West
Suite 200
P1B 2Y8

Telephone:
(705) 472-6500
Facsimile:
(705) 472-7760

ORILLIA, Ont.
279 Coldwater Road West
L3V 3M1

Telephone:
(705) 326-7605
Facsimile:
(705) 326-0837

PEACE RIVER, Alta.

10012 - 101st Street
Box 6030
T8S 1S1

Telephone:
(403) 624-3252
Facsimile:
(403) 624-8758

PORT COLBORNE, Ont.

92 Charlotte Street
Suite B
P.O. Box 336
L3K 5W1

Telephone:
(905) 834-3651
Facsimile:
(905) 834-5095

RICHMOND, B.C.

Suite 433
5811 Cooney Road
V6X 3M1

Telephone:
(604) 278-7159
Facsimile:
(604) 278-0359

ST. CATHARINES, Ont.

55 King Street
Suite 304
Box 2011
L2R 7R7

Telephone:
(905) 688-4822
Facsimile:
(905) 688-4837

SAINT JOHN, N.B.

55 Union Street
Suite 600
E2L 5B7

Telephone:
(506) 634-2900
Facsimile:
(506) 634-4569

ST. JOHN'S, Nfld.

187 Kenmount Road
P.O. Box 8037
A1B 3M7

Telephone:
(709) 722-5960
Facsimile:
(709) 722-7892

ST. STEPHEN, N.B.
Suite 201, Ganong Place
73 Milltown Blvd.
E3L 1G5

Telephone:
(506) 466-3291
Facsimile:
(506) 466-6310

SAULT STE. MARIE, Ont.
421 Bay Street
5th Floor
P6A 1X3

Telephone:
(705) 945-9700
Facsimile:
(705) 945-9705

SUMMERSIDE, P.E.I.
220 Water Street
Royal Bank Building
P.O. Box 1660
C1N 2V5

Telephone:
(902) 436-9155
Facsimile:
(902) 436-6913

SYDNEY, N.S.
Suite 200, George Place
500 George Street
B1P 1K6

Telephone:
(902) 562-5581
Facsimile:
(902) 562-0073

TILLSONBURG, Ont.
22 Harvey Street
P.O. Box 247
N4G 4H5

Telephone:
(519) 842-3604
Facsimile:
(519) 842-2178

TORONTO, Ont.
19th Floor, South Tower
Royal Bank Plaza
200 Bay Street, Box 55
M5J 2P9

Telephone:
(416) 366-0100
Facsimile:
(416) 360-4949

TRURO, N.S.
Suite 400
35 Commercial Street
P.O. Box 725
B2N 5E8

Telephone:
(902) 893-1150
Facsimile:
(902) 893-9757

VANCOUVER, B.C.

Suite 2800   Telephone:
1055 West Georgia Street   (604) 687-2711
P.O. Box 11177   Facsimile:
V6E 4N3   (604) 685-6569

VICTORIA, B.C.

Third Floor   Telephone:
888 Fort Street   (250) 383-4191
V8W 1H8   Facsimile:
                                    (250) 381-4623

WETASKIWIN, Alta.

5108-51st Avenue   Telephone:
T9A 0V2   (403) 352-1679
                                    Facsimile:
                                    (403) 352-2451

WINNIPEG, Man.

900 - One Lombard Place   Telephone:
R3B 0X3   (204) 944-0100
                                    Facsimile:
                                    (204) 957-5442

YARMOUTH, N.S.

328 Main Street   Telephone:
P.O. Box 297   (902) 742-7842
B5A 4B2   Facsimile:
                                    (902) 742-0224

Websites

Grant Thornton - www.GrantThornton.ca
Revenue Canada - www.rc.gc.ca

Index

With our compliments...

Send now for your complimentary subscription to *Catalyst*, Grant Thornton's newsletter focusing on business issues facing entrepreneurial businesses, owner-managers, and not-for-profit organizations. Fax this form to: *Catalyst*
Grant Thornton
Chartered Accountants/
Management Consultants
Fax: (416) 360-4944

Name: _____
Title: _____
Company: _____
Business Mailing Address: _____
_____

City: _____ Prov.: _____
Postal Code: _____
Business phone: (___) _____-_____
Business fax: (___) _____-_____
E-mail: _____

Type of business:
__ Private Corporation
__ Public Corporation
__ Proprietorship
__ Partnership
__ Limited Partnership
__ Joint Venture
__ Professional Practice

Ownership:
__ Owner-managed
__ Not owner-managed
__ Not-for-profit

Business description: _____
Check the most appropriate:
__ Agriculture and Fisheries
__ Business Services
__ Communications
__ Construction
__ Finance and Real Estate
__ Government
__ Health Care
__ High-technology Industries

__ Hospitality and Entertainment
__ Manufacturing and Distribution
__ Not-for-profit
__ Professional Services
__ Resource Industries
__ Transportation
__ Wholesale and Retail Trade

Number of employees: _____
Annual sales volume: _____